In *Film and Phenomenology: Toward a Realist Theory of Cinematic Representation,* Allan Casebier develops a theory of representation first indicated in the writings of Edmund Husserl, the father of phenomenology, and then applies it to the case of cinematic representation. This work provides a clear exposition of Husserl's highly influential but often obscure thought, as well as a demonstration of the power of phenomenology to illuminate the experience of cinema, the art form unique to the twentieth century.

Film and Phenomenology is intended as an antidote to all existing theories about the nature of cinematic representation, whether issuing from classic sources, such as the film theory of André Bazin, or from the poststructuralist synthesis of Lacanian psychoanalysis, Barthesean textual analysis, or Metzean cinesemiotics. Casebier shows how a phenomenological account of representation will further the aims of any film theory. Developing a viable feminist film theory, legitimizing the documentary, answering the challenge of Derridean deconstruction, and properly theorizing narrativity, *Film and Phenomenology* argues that theory of film must be realist both with respect to epistemology and ontological issues. In this way, this work runs contrary to the whole course of contemporary film theory, which has, to date, been deeply antirealist.

Albrecht Dürer's *Knight, Death, and the Devil.*

FILM AND PHENOMENOLOGY

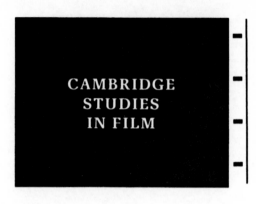

CAMBRIDGE STUDIES IN FILM

GENERAL EDITORS

Henry Breitrose, *Stanford University*
William Rothman, *University of Miami*

ADVISORY BOARD

Dudley Andrew, *University of Iowa*
Anthony Smith, *Magdalen College, Oxford*
Colin Young, *National Film School*

OTHER BOOKS IN THE SERIES

Paul Clark, *Chinese Cinema: Culture and Politics since 1949*

Paul Coates, *The Gorgon's Gaze: German Cinema, Expressionism, and the Image of Horror*

Sergei Eisenstein, *Nonindifferent Nature: Film and the Structure of Things* (trans. Herbert Marshall)

Vlada Petrić, *Constructivism in Film: The Man with the Movie Camera—A Cinematic Analysis*

Jean Renoir: *Renoir on Renoir: Interviews, Essays, and Remarks* (trans. Carol Volk)

Eric Rohmer: *The Taste for Beauty* (trans. Carol Volk)

William Rothman: *The "I" of the Camera: Essays in Film Criticism, History, and Aesthetics*

Paul Swann: *The British Documentary Film Movement, 1926–1946*

Trevor Whittock: *Metaphor and Film*

FILM AND PHENOMENOLOGY

Toward a Realist Theory of Cinematic Representation

ALLAN CASEBIER
Associate Professor, School of Cinema/Television
University of Southern California

The right of the
University of Cambridge
to print and sell
all manner of books
was granted by
Henry VIII in 1534.
The University has printed
and published continuously
since 1584.

CAMBRIDGE UNIVERSITY PRESS
CAMBRIDGE
NEW YORK PORT CHESTER MELBOURNE SYDNEY

CAMBRIDGE UNIVERSITY PRESS
Cambridge, New York, Melbourne, Madrid, Cape Town, Singapore, São Paulo, Delhi

Cambridge University Press
The Edinburgh Building, Cambridge CB2 8RU, UK

Published in the United States of America by Cambridge University Press, New York

www.cambridge.org
Information on this title: www.cambridge.org/9780521108546

First published 1991
This digitally printed version 2009

A catalogue record for this publication is available from the British Library

Library of Congress Cataloguing in Publication data
Casebier, Allan.
Film and phenomenology : Toward a realist theory of cinematic representation / Allan
Casebier.
   p.   cm. – (Cambridge studies in film)
Includes bibliographical references and index.
ISBN 0-521-41132-7 (hardcover)
1. Motion pictures – Philosophy.   2. Husserl, Edmund, 1859–1938   3. Phenomenology.
   I. Title.   II. Series
PN1995.C364   1991
791.43′01 – dc20   91–13678

ISBN 978-0-521-41132-5 hardback
ISBN 978-0-521-10854-6 paperback

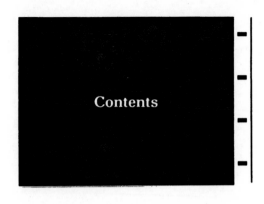

Contents

Acknowledgments

Thanks are due to members of the Society for the Study of Husserl's Philosophy who shared their considerable knowledge of phenomenology – J. N. Mohanty, Peter McCormick, Barry Smith, David Woodruff Smith, Ron McIntyre, Izchak Miller, Arthur Szylewicz, Martin Schwab, and especially my colleague at the University of Southern California, Dallas Willard. In preparing the manuscript, thanks are due to Owen Costello and Jeanette Mitrano. Bill Rothman provided excellent guidance in drawing the manuscript together and comments on its content.

I also thank the editors and publishers of the following journals for their permission to reprint, in revised form, portions of the following articles of mine:

"Burch's Theory of Japanese Cinema," *Millennium Film Journal,* nos. 14–15, 35–41.

"A Deconstructive Documentary," *Journal of Film and Video,* 40 (Winter 1988), 34–9.

"Idealist and Realist Theories of the Documentary," *Post-Script,* 6(1)(Fall 1986), 66–75.

"Oshima in Contemporary Theoretical Perspective," *Wide Angle,* 9(2)(1987), 4–17.

"The Phenomenology of Japanese Cinema: Husserlian Intervention in the Theory of Cinematic Representation," *Quarterly Review of Film and Video,* 12(3) (1990), 9–19. Courtesy Harwood Academic Publishers GmbH.

"Representation of Reality and Reality of Representation in Contemporary Film Theory," *Persistence of Vision,* no. 5 (Spring 1987), 36–43.

"Transparency, Transaction, and Transcendence: Husserl's Middle Road to Cinematic Representation," *Husserl Studies,* 5 (1988), 127–41. © Kluwer Academic Publishers. Reprinted by permission of Kluwer Academic Publishers.

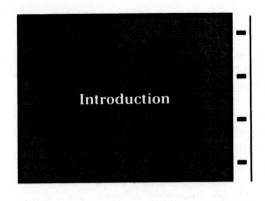

Introduction

At the bedrock of any theory of film must be a viable account of cinematic representation. The view that a theorist holds about those experiences in which an audience apprehends what a motion picture depicts and/or portrays and/or symbolizes affects everything that is said subsequently in the film theory.* An adequate account of cinematic representation is yet to be developed. It will be the effort of this work to correct this situation. The effects of having had inadequate theories of cinematic representation on which to ground film theory may be felt in the deepest recesses of writing about film.

In conceptualizing cinematic representation, theorists must be alive to underlying epistemological and ontological grounds for their theories. In contemporary film theory this crucial dimension of philosophical activity had been absent. *Ontology* is the inquiry into the nature of being and existence. *Epistemology* is the inquiry into *knowledge* of being and existence. In each of these inquiries choices have to be made among possible positions, and justification has to be given for the choices. In contemporary film theory these conditions have not been satisfied. Where the underlying epistemological and ontological issues have been perceived, no really sound justifications for the chosen grounds have been forthcoming.

For example, contemporary film theory has unquestioningly been idealist with respect to epistemological grounds. An idealist holds that how the world is and how we know it are dependent on the activity of the knowing mind. Realism is the opposing position in a long-standing debate.[2] The realist holds that how the world is exists independently of the knowing mind. For contemporary film theory, with its

---

* In this discussion, Monroe Beardsley's[1] proposal for the use of the family of terms designating various types of represention will be followed. *Depiction* is representation of a type of object (e.g., Murnau's *Nosferatu, A Symphony of Horrors* [*Nosferatu – Eine Symphonie, des Grauens*] depicts a vampire). *Portrayal* is representation of an individual (e.g., Murnau's *Nosferatu* portrays Count Orlock). *Symbolizing* is representation via suggested, not literal, meaning (e.g., in Herzog's *Nosferatu, the Vampire* [*Nosferatu – Phantom der Nacht*], the German soul is symbolized by the vampire figure).

1

deep commitment to an unquestioned idealist account of cinematic representation, what a motion picture depicts, portrays, or symbolizes depends on the spectator's language, ideological beliefs, aesthetic sensibilities, unconscious processes, and so forth. According to idealism, none of the objects, real or fictional, depicted in, for instance, *Citizen Kane* exist independently of that motion picture or of the acts of spectators in apprehending them. This is so because our ideas about human life, early twentieth-century life, and of William Randolph Hearst govern an apprehension of the objects represented by the film; these objects do not exist independently of cinematic or other representations of our own subjectivity. Moreover, Charles Foster Kane as a fictional character is merely a construction out of the elements in our experience of the film (out of the visuals and sounds we experience at a screening of the film), not an entity existing independently of our acts of apprehending it.

As we shall see, both realist and idealist accounts of cinematic representation may be found in the history of film theory. Unfortunately, efforts to develop a realist model for cinematic representation have been, up to this time, largely unsuccessful. André Bazin is the most prominent exponent of realism.[3] His account, depending as it does on a notion of transparent relationship between camera and the real, has been justly rejected by film theory for its inability to take into account paradigm cases of cinematic representation. Though more sophisticated versions of realism that are critical of transparency accounts may be formulated, these have not been forthcoming – until this work. Into the void created by the failure of Bazin's realist model for cinematic representation have rushed a number of idealist theories of representation that obtrude upon a proper understanding of film experience because of the very idealism that is at their core.

With respect to ontology, contemporary film theory has adopted a nominalist rather than a realist position. In ontology, a theorist must hold either that only particulars exist or that particulars and universals exist. Contemporary film theory has opted for there being only particulars with spectators' constructive activity providing the cinematic representations. In linking the nominalist ontology of Nelson Goodman to the analysis of cinematic representation, J. Dudley Andrew says: "There is no primary real world which we subsequently subject to various types of representation [Goodman contends]. Rather it makes far more sense to speak of multiple worlds which individuals construct."[4]

There is a received wisdom about the short history of film theory. First there was a so-called classic period comprised of individual efforts to provide a totalizing picture of the nature of the motion picture medium (Munsterberg, Eisenstein, Pudovkin, Arnheim, Balázs, Kra-

cauer, Bazin, etc.). Second there was a so-called contemporary movement, starting some time in the 1960s – the events of May 1968 are
always mentioned as profoundly effecting the movement – which per-
sists into the 1990s.

This contemporary movement has involved many currents from the
beginnings to the present, interweaving patterns, temporary amalgams,
common purposes: Barthesian textual analysis, Althussearean Marxism, Lacanian psychoanalysis, Metzean semiotics, poststructuralist
synthesis, and so forth. Cinesemiotics gave way to psychoanalytic-
semiotics, structuralism gave way to poststructuralism, and so forth.
Entering the 1990s one finds a bewildering array of activities coexis-
tent within the field. Feminist film theory holds a preeminent position,
but there is vitality in ideological criticism, cultural studies, narrative
theory, psychoanalytic criticism, even auteur studies. At first there was
a unity felt in rejection of a prior form of criticism with a humanistic
orientation. Now, no unity seems to bind the movement. The contemporary movement seems at a crossroads, seeking an identity, a successful approach, ways around theoretical blockages. What is required
for film theory to gain its bearings is the presentation of a viable realist account. For the idealist/nominalist, framework, not always acknowledged as such (many theorists think they are presenting "mate-
rialist" theories), is what is holding back the field.

One can hardly read a page of film theory without feeling the ever-
present idealist/nominalist framework. Some examples should suffice:

The really important breakthrough . . . came in the rejection of the traditional
idea of a work as primarily a representation of something else, whether an
idea of the real world, and the concentration of attention on the text of the
work itself and on signs from which it was constructed.   – Peter Wollen[5]

Instead of seeing the activity of our own perception and the construction of an
image's meaning, we see through our perceptual habit and the image's construction to an already meaningful world (without, in this case, "seeing
through" the deception that is involved, the actual production or fabrication of
meaning).   – Bill Nichols[6]

Narration is a product of both a narrator and a reader; just as the text must
create (inscribe) its reader, so a reader must create the text in its telling.
                                                              – Edward Branigan[7]

Before a proper mode of representation or aesthetic relation to the "real" can
be established, we have to have some idea of where the "real" itself is located,
and how, if at all, we can have knowledge of it. At issue then is the status of
"lived experience," of phenomenal appearances, their relation to underlying
structures, the determining role of "signification" in production of the real,
and the place of consciousness in this production.   – Christine Gledhill[8]

By woman, I mean a fictional construct, a distillate from diverse but congruent discourses dominant in Western cultures...which works as both their vanishing point and their specific condition of existence.   – Teresa de Lauretis[9]

The text is not something "out there," an autonomous or completed source of meaning and value. Instead it is seen as a field, a site, a location, a confluence of technology, ideology, and the codes of representation.   – Beverle Houston[10]

A poetics – derived from poiesis or "active making" – puts at the center of its concerns the problem of how art works are constructed.... In the process of narration, various aspects of the film become cues for spectatorial activity. Of these cues, the most salient are those proffered by the syuzhet, the substance and sequence of narrative events explicitly presented in the film.... The syuzhet prompts the spectator to build the fabula, or total system of story events.
    – David Bordwell[11]

    As will become apparent, enormous conceptual difficulties plague the idealist/nominalist account of representation. Once one realizes the commitment of contemporary film theories to idealism/nominalism, one understands why adequate answers have not been forthcoming to fundamental questions of cinema, such as: What form should a feminist film theory take? What legitimacy if any does the documentary form have? How shall cinematic sound be conceptualized in relationship to images? What relationship exists between narrative and underlying ideological belief? These questions of cinema cannot be dealt with until the underlying idealist/nominalist theory of cinematic representation is expunged and replaced by a viable realist theory of cinematic representation that unearths the actual process involved in grasping what a motion picture represents.

    Phenomenology provides the needed realist framework. Edward Husserl's phenomenological method for understanding the nature of perception and his theory of artistic representation, as extended and developed here, will illuminate the experience of film representation in a way not found previously in film theory. The phenomenological method, in Husserl's theory as practice, is a way of looking at the same time at both subject and object in the cognitive act while maintaining *the* object of the act as existing independently. Etymologically, phenomenology is the logic of phenomena. What we know of the world (including cinematic representation) has to do with our experience of phenomena, that is, the way things appear to us. There is a logic to the way consciousness relates to appearances in its acts, how it contributes to their constitution, how the appearances thus constituted mediate our apprehension of *the* object of the experience while leaving unaffected *the* object of the experience.

    Whereas Bazin's unfruitful realist theory does not make proper room for *mediation* in the process of apprehending representations, Husserlian phenomenology develops a highly sophisticated analysis of the role of consciousness in grasping an art object such as a film. Whereas Bazinian realism relies on transparency as central to the analysis of cinematic representation, phenomenology rejects transparency.

Whereas idealism makes the acts of consciousness actually determine the nature of, for example, a man's life, the fictional character Charles Foster Kane, or the parodied William Randolph Hearst, the phenomenological method allows us to recognize how these represented objects remain as they are, unaffected by our acts of consciousness, while mediation nevertheless obtains.

As we shall see, Husserlian analysis offers a realist epistemology by means of which we come to realize that *the* object of our perceptual acts in an experience of a film *constrains* or *limits* the direction of our consciousness in the act of apprehending representation. When we experience *Citizen Kane,* we do not have the kind of absolute freedom that contemporary film theory posits; when it takes spectators' acts in experiencing a film to be constitutive of *the* very object of perception.

Edmund Husserl (1859–1938) is properly described as the father of phenomenology. His influence on the course of thought in Continental philosophy in the twentieth century can scarcely be exaggerated. From the work of his most famous student, Martin Heidegger, through the existentialist philosophical movement, his influence is of the first importance. Kurt Gödel and Hermann Weyl ranked Husserl as the greatest philosopher since Leibniz.[12] Bertrand Russell described *Logical Investigations* (1901) as "monumental."[13] Though the work of other phenomenologists (e.g., Heidegger, Merleau-Ponty, Sartre) can no doubt illuminate film experience as well, the focus in this book will be on the theory of artistic and cinematic representation as it issues from a Husserlian perspective. Husserl's two early major works, *Logical Investigations* and *Ideas* (1913), will be the focus here.[14]

Ever since the publication of Husserl's major early works, there has been much interest among his followers in the contribution that a Husserlian conceptual framework can make to a variety of intellectual endeavors, but it has rarely been applied to the theory of film. Husserl's ideas have remained largely unavailable outside the small circle of Husserlian scholarship. No doubt an important reason has been the forbidding language in which Husserl framed his theories. Taking this problem into account, it will be a major effort herein to explain Husserl's analyses of representation in ways understandable to all readers.

As with many terms in a living language, the term 'phenomenology' is used in more than one way. J. Dudley Andrew, for instance, in speaking of the sources for hermeneutics in phenomenology, claims that:

> Stemming as it does from phenomenological roots, hermeneutics must clearly oppose any objectivist notion of truth or of the text. The point of departure for phenomenologists is not the text but rather the act of reading or interjecting. Indeed, they would surely assert that the text exists only as read and that [E. D.] Hirsch's program to discover the meaning of the pristine text, as it exists unread and eternal, is altogether phantasmic.[15]

Contrast this characterization of phenomenology with that of Husserl, the founder of the movement:

> Truth for this or that species, e.g., for the human species is ... an absurd mode of speech.... What is true is absolutely, intrinsically true: truth is one and the same, whether men or non-men, angels or gods apprehend and judge it. (*LI*, 140)

> Colors, Tones, Triangles, etc., always have the essential properties of Colors, Tones, Triangles, etc., whether anyone in the world knows such a fact or not. (*LI*, 165)

Though realism as epistemological doctrine differs from realism as ontological doctrine, there is an important link between the two for the phenomenological analysis developed here. In holding that how representation is does not depend on the activities of the knowing mind, Husserl held also that there exist universals that the spectators apprehend and utilize in recognizing what a work of art represents. Husserl's anticonstructionist stance with respect to our knowledge of representation is bound up with his contention that universals are exemplified in representations. We may know what an art object represents partly because we are able to grasp the instantiation of universals. The linking to be found in Husserlian phenomenology of these epistemological and ontological realisms will be followed here in developing a phenomenological theory of cinematic representation.

We shall start with an initial exposition of Husserl's theory of artistic representation, with illustrations of how it would be utilized to analyze representation in the motion picture. We shall compare and contrast Husserl's ontological position with the insupportable nominalism underlying contemporary film theory. Then we shall show that, even when theorists (e.g., Jean-Louis Baudry, J. Dudley Andrew, Gaylyn Studlar) have attempted to use Husserl's theory, they have inadvertently misrepresented it as an idealist theory of cinematic representation.[16] It has not only been characteristic of film theorist commentary on Husserl that he be viewed as an idealist, but a substantial portion of Husserl scholarship has had a similar thrust.[17] In Chapter I, on Husserl's central concept on the noema, a defense of a realist interpretation of Husserl will be presented.

Contemporary film theory rests upon grounds that cannot support it. It is the overall thesis of this book that the Husserlian model preserves the genuine insights of prior theories while avoiding their problems. It provides a solid foundation upon which fruitful approaches to the fundamental questions of cinema may be constituted. The advantages of a phenomenology of filmic representation will be developed vis-à-vis image, sound, narrative, documentary, content, and reception.

Notes

1. Monroe Beardsley, *Aesthetics: Problems in the Philosophy of Criticism* (New York: Harcourt Brace, 1958), Part VI, "Representations in the Visual Arts," pp. 267–93.

2. R. J. Hirst, "Realism," in Paul Edwards, *The Encyclopedia of Philosophy* (New York: Collier-Macmillan, 1967), vol. 7, p. 77.

3. The major film theoretical work of André Bazin is *What is Cinema? Vol. I*, trans. Hugh Gray (Berkeley: University of California Press, 1967).

4. J. Dudley Andrew, *Concepts in Film Theory* (Oxford: Oxford University Press, 1985), p. 38.

5. Peter Wollen, *Signs and Meaning in the Cinema*, 3rd ed. (Bloomington: Indiana University Press, 1972), p. 161.

6. Bill Nichols, *Ideology and the Image: Social Representation in the Cinema and Other Media* (Bloomington: Indiana University Press, 1981), pp. 35–6.

7. Edward Branigan, "Subjectivity under Siege: From Fellini's 8½ to Oshima's *The Story of the Man Who Left His Will on Film*," *Screen*, 19(1) (Spring 1978), 27.

8. Christine Gledhill, "Recent Developments in Feminist Film Criticism," in Mary Ann Doane, Linda Williams, and Patricia Mellencamp, (eds.), *Re-Vision* (Frederick, Md.: University Press of America, 1984), p. 5.

9. Teresa de Lauretis, *Alice Doesn't: Feminism, Semiotics, Cinema* (Bloomington: Indiana University Press, 1984), p. 5.

10. Beverle Houston, "An Old New Critic Look at the New Discourse," Annual Meeting, MLA, Los Angeles, 1983.

11. David Bordwell, *Ozu and the Poetics of Cinema* (Princeton: Princeton University Press, 1989), pp. 51–2.

12. G. C. Rota, "A Husserl Perspective," *Occasional Review*, no. 2 (Autumn 1974), p. 100.

13. Bertrand Russell, *Sceptical Essays* (New York: Norton, 1928), p. 100.

14. Hereafter, abbreviated *LI* and *I*, respectively.

15. J. Dudley Andrew, *Concepts in Film Theory* (Oxford: Oxford University Press, 1984), p. 178. For other characterizations of phenomenology unconnected with Husserl's concept of the "method," see Christian Metz, "On the Idealist Theory of the Cinema," in *The Imaginary Signifier: Psychoanalysis*

and the Cinema, trans. C. Britton, A. Williams, B. Brewster, and A. Guzzetti (Bloomington: Indiana University Press, 1977), pp. 52–6.

16. Jean-Louis Baudry, "Ideological Effects of the Basic Cinematographic Apparatus," *Cinéthique,* nos. 7–8 (1970), trans. Alan Williams, first printed in *Film Quarterly,* 28(2), (Winter 1974–5). Gaylin Studlar, "Reconciling Feminism and Phenomenology: Notes on Problems and Possibilities, Texts and Contexts," *Quarterly Review of Film and Video,* Special Issue "Phenomenology and Film," July 1990.

17. See Aron Gurwitsch, *The Field of Consciousness* (Pittsburgh: University of Duquesne Press, 1964).

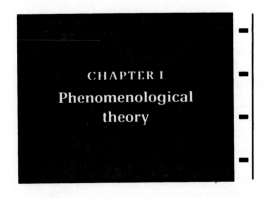

CHAPTER I

Phenomenological theory

Husserl's theory of artistic representation

In explaining his theory of artistic representation, Husserl utilizes Albrecht Dürer's engraving *Knight, Death, and the Devil* (see frontispiece) as illustration. He provides an account of the acts in which perceivers engage when they recognize what is represented by the engraving. It is Husserl's view that a flesh and blood knight is depicted by the engraving. As he puts it:

> We are observing Dürer's engraving, "The Knight, Death, and the Devil." We distinguish ... the perceptive consciousness in which, within the black, colorless lines, there appear to us the figures of the "knight on his horse," "death," and the "devil." We do not turn our attention to these in aesthetic contemplation as objects. We rather turn our attention to the realities presented in the picture – more precisely stated, to the "depictured" realities, to the flesh and blood knight, etc. (*I*, §111)[1]

Thus, a cornerstone of Husserl's realist account of artistic representation is the capacity of perceivers to *transcend* their perceptual acts in recognizing what an art object such as the Dürer engraving depicts. In the case of the Dürer, the flesh and blood knight is a real knight existing independently of the spectator's perceptual act of grasping that he is the object represented by the engraving. He is not produced by the activity of the perceiver of the engraving. That he is *the* object represented by the engraving is *discoverable* by perceivers.

An example will illustrate how Husserl's theory would apply to the case of apprehending cinematic representations. In recognizing what de Sica's *Shoeshine* (*Sciuscia*) represents, Italian boys would be some of the depicted objects. The depicted Italian boys exist independently of our conscious acts of apprehending them as depicted objects. In one sequence we see two particular Italian boys, Giuseppe and Pasquale, sentenced to serve time in jail. These two fictionally portrayed characters also exist independently of our consciousness as we apprehend their representation. A symbolic object of the motion picture, freedom, also has an existence independent of our consciousness and of the motion picture. That is, the flesh and blood reality of immediate postwar Italian society, its young males, and freedom exist independently of the de Sica motion picture and our conscious acts of grasping them. Late-1940s Italian society (or, for that matter, the flesh and blood knight in the Dürer work) is not created or constructed by spectator activity.

By contrast, for contemporary film theory, the objects depicted, portrayed, and symbolized by an art object (whether a film or an engraving) are constructions made by perceivers. Sensations are the material used in this constructive activity; shared assumptions, expectations, codes, and so forth are the tools perceivers utilize in accomplishing the constructions. The depicted objects (e.g., the knight in the Dürer example) do not exist independently of the art object; most certainly they do not exist independently of the perceptual acts of perceivers, whose acts actually constitute them.

In this idealist vein, Bill Nichols writes about the nature of everyday life perception and perception of artistic representation:

The habitual or coded nature of perception obscures our own active role in perception and that obscuring is now compounded by the object-status of the image.... Photographic realism...works to naturalize comprehension; it hides the work of perceiving meaning behind the mask of a naturally, obviously meaningful image. This reinforcement...is ideological in its implication that the surfaces of things are already meaningful, that this meaning is objectively given rather than a social construct.[2]

Nichols elaborates the idealist view (that the nature of the things we perceive depends on the constructive activity of the mind) in the following passage:

Our perception of the physical world is...based on codes involving iconic signs. The world does not enter our mind nor does it deposit a picture of itself there spontaneously. Perception depends on coding the world into iconic signs that can represent it within our mind. The force of the apparent identity is enormous, however. We think that it is the world itself we see in our "mind's eye," rather than a coded picture of it.... Hence both cinema and perception itself share a common coding process involving iconic signs.[3]

The view that Nichols is urging is that consciousness, in knowing the world and the objects represented by photography, utilizes codes in constructing what it perceives. Though a process of naturalizing comprehension makes it seem that represented objects are objectively given, they really are only social constructs.

In approaching the question of the nature of artistic and cinematic representation, it might seem obvious that there are at least two types. Holbein's portrait of Henry VIII has the real-life individual Henry VIII, the king of England, as the object represented *by* the painting. By contrast, if we wake up one winter morning in our New England cottage and the frost on the window seems to take on the shape of Henry VIII's face we see Henry VIII *in* the frost.

For contemporary theory, this latter case – representation *in* – has been made paradigmatic of all representation; that is, it is as if perceivers only read meanings into what they see. Whereas representation *by* is suppressed; representation is not depiction or portrayal or symbolizing of an object existing independently of my mind as in realism. When I see something represented in a work of art, I read it into that work; I do not discover what independently existing object is represented by the work.

Mediation

Husserl's core insight is that the depicted objects and events of a work of art exist independently of appreciators' perceptual acts in apprehending what is represented. He elaborates on this view by saying that apprehension of the knight as the object represented by the Dürer engraving depends on an apprehension of features of what appears to us in perceiving the engraving: "Within the black, colorless lines" as Husserl puts it, are what he calls small gray figures (the "knight on his horse," "death," and "the devil"). Our act of being aware of these appearances is the foundation of (is the condition for) our act of recognizing the real knight as the depicted object. In the experience of apprehending *Shoeshine*, what appears to us as we experience the performances of the boy actors *founds* (is a condition of)* our recognition that Italian boys are depicted, Giuseppe and Pasquale as well as Italian society is portrayed, and freedom is symbolized.

Husserlian phenomenology thus analyzes representation in terms of the *experience* of an art object, not simply in terms of a relationship between some object within the work of art and some object in the world, for example, not as a relation such as that between an icon and an object that it resembles. It is relationship between experiences of certain sorts that is the source for the representation. In this way, as

* In Husserl's theory, "found" may be characterized as follows: An experience of an object *O* is founded on an experience of another object *C* only if the experience of *O* could not be intentionally related to *O* unless the experience of *C* occurred. Thus, the act of living through the appearances of the small gray figures in the Dürer engraving is a condition of apprehending the real knight as the object of the act of recognizing what the engraving represents.

we shall see, Husserl would be able to get around the objections to Bazinian realism in film theory. Husserl can acknowledge that there is no iconic or indexical relationship between the art object and the object represented yet hold that representation is nevertheless realist.

In analyzing the highly mediated way in which what appears to us in the art gallery and at a screening of a film such as *Shoeshine*, Husserl introduces the technical terms 'noema,' 'noesis,' 'hyletic,' 'apperception,' and 'horizon.' In order to appreciate the complexity, sophistication, and power of Husserl's account of representation, it will be necessary to understand these difficult concepts, a matter to which we now turn.

Noema and noesis

Husserl uses technical terms such as 'noema' because many preconceptions attach to words ordinarily used in talking about perception and consciousness. A term such as 'appearance' has become so encrusted with associations that it is difficult to use it in setting out a new way of thinking about long-standing epistemological and ontological problems. Husserl goes back to the Greeks to find a term that has the capacity to reorient his readers' understanding.

In every act of perception, it is Husserl's view that there are three *moments,* which obtain simultaneously – noematic, noetic, and hyletic. These moments *arise together* as we perceive the object of our experience.

The term *noema* (plural, *noemata*) is a transliteration from a Greek term (*noein*) for thought, understanding, or perception. It emphasizes the product or medium of thinking; concepts, notions, or appearances. In the Husserlian system, noemata found (are a condition of) our apprehension of the object of our perception.

In the experience of the Dürer engraving, several noemata become formed. The appearances of the small gray figures are noemata. In the case of *Shoeshine,* we will see that the appearances of the Italian nonactors (e.g., how they look, how their faces are lit, etc.) as they go off to jail are noemata.

The process of mediation also involves noesis. Though drawn from the same Greek verb (*noew*) as noema, *noesis* emphasizes the process or mental act in which an object is apprehended. Noeses are the various ways in which the mind positions itself in relation to objects in order to know them.[4]

In the case of the Dürer engraving, the act of having the appearances of the small figures *guide* and *constrain* our perception of the real knight, death, and the devil constitutes the operation of noesis. With respect to *Shoeshine,* we reach beyond what appears to us as we attend to the performances, mise-en-scène, and so forth, to apprehend Italian boys, postwar Italian society, and freedom in a way founded on the appearances, the noemata.

The third phase of the mediation process is what Husserl calls 'the hyletic' (*I*, §85). Hyletic data are what in Anglo–American philosophy have often been called 'sensa.'[5] When we experience *Shoeshine*, we sense line, pattern, size and shape relationships, camera movement, camera placement, editing forms, sound textures, and so forth. In film experience, these features are hyletic data. The hyletic data experienced in looking at the Dürer engraving (the sensa correspond to shapes, volumes, etc.) are sources for the founding of the apprehension of the real knight.

Apprehension of the flesh and blood knight as *the* object represented by the engraving is founded not only on apprehension of these hyletic data but also on the appearances of the small gray figures. In identifying the mode of apprehension in which this process occurs, Husserl utilizes the concept of apperception.

Apperception

Apperception[6] is a mode of apprehension different from perception but intimately bound up with it. When a perceiver apperceives, he or she "lives through" or "passes through" the sensa (or other object) without making them objects of perception. Suppose I wear eyeglasses. An object is coming toward me at an ever-quickening pace, which I notice through my eyeglasses. Suppose also that I notice a smudge on my eyeglasses. I can focus on the on-rushing object, *passing through* (apperceiving) the eyeglass and its smudged surface, or I can shift attention to the smudge on the surface, making that smudge *the* object of my attention. Similarly, when attending a lecture, I might focus on the sound of the speaker's voice – its timbre, pitch, inflection, attitudinal "tone" – or simply live through it, experience it apperceptively, and make the meaning of what is being said the object of my action.

Thus, perceivers of the Dürer engraving can make sensa of the engraving – line, shape, proportion, and so forth – the objects of their perception. However, in the act of grasping what the engraving depicts, they live through or pass through the sensa in order to grasp what the engraving represents, the real knight. They pass through the hyletic data; the data are not objects of perception the way the knight is. In recognizing what is represented in the Dürer, we pass through line, shape, size, and so forth to apprehend the knight who exists independently of the engraving. In recognizing what *Shoeshine* represents, we pass through line, shape, camera placement, editing relationships, acting, sound quality, and so forth to grasp the flesh and blood Italian boys of postwar Italian society.

The act of apprehending what the engraving represents is also founded in turn on the apprehension of the appearances of the small gray figures, an apprehension that is apperceptive in nature. It is at this point that the complex interaction of elements in the Husserlian system becomes palpable. The appearances of these small figures are the noemata; these noemata function in our consciousness as we apprehend what the engraving represents. The noemata are objects of apperception; the real knight is *the* object of the perception, the perceptual act as a whole. Apprehension of the appearances of the small figures mediates the grasping of *the* object represented.

In our *Shoeshine* example, a double process of passing through, apperceiving, occurs. In the first moment, we pass through the hyletic data – camera placement, actor's gestures, sound quality, and so forth – to grasp what appears to us (the boy actors performing), the noemata, which for contemporary film theory are alleged to function as signs from which as Peter Wollen puts it, "the [film] text was constructed." We have seen Nichols speak of how we "think it is the world itself we see...rather than a coded picture of it....Both cinema and perception itself share a common coding process." In another place, Nichols argues that:

The existential bond establishing the indexical aspect of the cinematic sign system provides a powerful inducement to awe...so much so that it is easy to forget completely that we are dealing with a sign system rather than a direct, unmediated duplication of reality.[7]

Though in the perceptual act in question the real knight is *the* object of perception, it should not be thought that such an object is a necessary terminus. It has often been thought, for example, that Dürer's knight symbolizes human existence. Francis Russell writes the following about the Dürer engraving and its symbolic meaning:

In *Knight, Death, and the Devil*, Dürer has presented the embodiment of the Christian resolution, the knight who makes his way to his goal in defiance of Death and Hell. The scene is a forbidding wilderness, the Devil a swine-snouted monster with bat's wings and a single horn. Death is no longer a skeleton but a sad-eyed, decaying corpse without lips or nose, who holds up an hourglass as he swings his sorry nag athwart the path. The knight rides straight ahead, impervious, his face stern under the raised visor of his helmet.... The formidable figure advancing along the abyss of life, contemptuous of lurking perils becomes the essence of human courage. Generations have found this quality in the engraving. The anti-Christian philosopher, Friedrich

Nietzche, despite his conviction, saw the knight as a "symbol of our existence."[8]

In order to apprehend what the engraving represents (in the sense of symbolizes), perceivers of the engraving need to live through, apperceive, the knight in the process of grasping the fate of humanity as the symbolized object.

In *Shoeshine*, the white horse symbolizes freedom. In grasping freedom as the symbolized object, perceivers of the film pass not only through an awareness of qualities such as camera placement, editing form, sound quality, and so forth, through the appearances of the white horse, but also pass through the white horse as a flesh and blood creature and their conscious act of knowing that creature.

Moreover, Husserl thinks there is something special about the nature of the perceptual act involved in apprehending artistic representation, something not involved in nonart cases. In apprehending art objects, perceivers put aside the question of whether what they experience exists or not, or as he puts it, exists in any other positional modality.

We set aside the existential question to focus instead on how the appearances that we are aware of *guide* us to some other object, not here present, without regard for whether that other object exists or not. *Neutrality modification* is the term Husserl uses. As he puts it:

That which makes the depicting [in the Dürer engraving] possible and mediates it, namely, the consciousness, of the "picture" of the small gray figures ...is now an example for the neutrality-modification of the picture. This depicting picture-object stands before us neither as being nor as non-being, nor in any other positional modality. (*I*, §111)

Intentionality

It is characteristic of the Husserlian system that consciousness is always consciousness *of* something. Husserl uses the term 'intend' or 'intentional' to mark this relationship. 'Intention' in this sense is derived from the Latin term *intentio* meaning extending or stretching out to. The real knight is *intended* as the object of the perceptual act of recognizing what the engraving represents. Noesis gives the intentional direction, the ofness of the act, to the sensa. Without this intentional direction, the sensa would not mean anything to the perceiver.

Were we to consider how intentionality is present in the experience of *Shoeshine*, we may take the recognition of the white horse as a depicted object. The lines, shapes, camera placement, sound texture, and so forth, which are the sensa, the hyletic data, would be meaningless unless noesis gives them an intentional direction. The noemata become formed, something appears to us – an appearance of a white horse – together with a reaching beyond our perceptual act to a flesh and blood horse. The noesis, the ofness of the act, is founded on an awareness of the sensa. It is not the case, as the idealist would have it, that the white horse is constructed by the perceiver out of the sensa.

For Husserl, the process of reaching beyond – intentionality – involves a complex interaction between what appears to us and our manner of positioning ourselves in being aware of it.

The appearances at one stage make possible all of the various subsequent directions of consciousness from the hyletic data through the appearances of the small figures (the noemata), through the knight to the fate of humanity if attention is directed to the symbolic subject. Husserl would say that insofar as we are recognizing the white horse in *Shoeshine* as a symbol of freedom, (1) we are *constrained* to take what appears to us (founded on sensa) as reaching beyond to a real object – a real white horse – existing independently of the motion picture and (2) we are *constrained* by the awareness of that object reached out to, the real white horse, to reach still further beyond to freedom. As we watch the interaction of subject and object, we realize that the film bombards the subject with sensa; the subject in turn allows itself to be *constrained* to reach beyond in response to what appears to the subject.

Reduction

Husserl introduces the method of reduction in order to promote understanding of the essential features of experience. It proceeds by turning our inquiry away from the objects of our acts and turning our attention toward the acts themselves in order that we may discover the structures that mediate intentionality. In bracketing, we bracket in the first place our natural standpoint toward objects, that is, the intentional posture we usually assume in everyday life; we put aside presuppositions and habitual ways of conceiving things that might otherwise obscure our understanding.

Our natural standpoint in relation to de Sica's *Shoeshine* is to take the motion picture as an object in the world like many others. He illustrates the natural standpoint and its bracketing with the example of perceiving an apple tree:

Let us suppose that we are looking with pleasure in a garden at a blossoming apple-tree, at the fresh young green of the lawn, and so forth. The perception and the pleasure that accompanies it is obviously not that which at the same time is perceived and gives pleasure.

. . .

From the natural standpoint, the apple-tree is something that exists in the transcendent reality of space, and the perception as well as the pleasure [is] a psychical state which we enjoy as real human beings. (*I*, §88)

The object of the perceptual act – the apple tree – exists independently of the perceptual act, that is, its existence transcends the act, having its existence in real space. The perception is, on the other hand, a psychical state had by a real human being; human perceivers exist also independently of any of their particular states of consciousness, for example, perception, introspection, memory, imagination, and so forth. Husserl says that "between . . . the real man or the real perception on the one hand, and the real apple-tree on the other hand, there subsist real relations" (*I*, §88).

The method of reduction permits us to look, at the same time, at both subject and object in the act of perception. In apprehending the white horse as a depicted object in *Shoeshine*, we turn our attention away from the object of our acts, that is, the motion picture as an object understandable in terms of scientific and commonsense notions – celluloid, an instance of entertainment – to focus on the acts themselves involved in perceiving it (*I*, §56a.). We bracket, we set aside, the motion picture as understood from the natural standpoint in order to realize what happens in the act of perception. The essential features of the process of perception are, by their very nature, not noticed while they are happening.

Whereas the idealist would reduce statements about what *Shoeshine* depicts (e.g., a white horse) to statements about subjects constructing of the white horse out of sensa using codes, Husserl would counsel the use of the reduction to notice how we pass through the sensa, how we permit ourselves to reach beyond what appears to us, to intend a real white horse without noticing in the perceptual act that we are doing it.

The reduction takes three forms: phenomenological, transcendental, and eidetic. In the *phenomenological* (or psychological) reduction, the aim is to focus attention on consciousness and its experiences while correspondingly turning attention away from external objects. In *transcendentally* reducing, an elimination of empirical or naturalistic assumptions about the stream of consciousness occurs. In the *eidetic* reduction (*eidetic* derives from *eidos*, meaning essence), there occurs a generalizing of the results attained through a transcendental study of consciousness. Reduction is to be taken as a way of narrowing down the scope of inquiry. In no way does it involve the elimination of one element in favor of others, for example, in a reduction of objects to sense-data (*I*, chap. 6).

In introducing the reduction into the analysis, Husserl has been noting the possibility of a nonveridical experience in the case of the perception of the apple tree:

In certain cases it may be that the perception is a "mere hallucination"; and that the perceived, this apple-tree that stands before us, does not exist in the "real" objective world ... nothing remains but the perception; there is nothing real out there to which it relates. (*I*, §88b)

Husserl is calling attention to the fact that even though the experience may have been, for example, a hallucination, we still perceived a definite something. By utilizing the reduction, we focus on the perceived as such apart from its relationship to independently existing objects. The transcendental world is said to enter its bracket (*I*, §88b). With the suspension provided by the reduction, Husserl says:

A relation between perception and perceived (as likewise between the pleasure and that which pleases) is obviously left over, a relationship which in its essential nature comes before us in "pure immanence," purely that is on the ground of the phenomenologically reduced experience of perception and pleasure. (*I*, §88b)

Husserl then emphasizes that:

Even the phenomenologically reduced perceptual experience is a perception *of* "this apple-tree in bloom in this garden, and so forth," and likewise the reduced pleasure, a pleasure of what is thus perceived. (*I*, §88c)

Upon noticing the residue after performing the reduction, a crucial question may now be asked:

From our phenomenological standpoint we can and must put the question of essence. What is the perceived-as-such? What essential phases does it harbor in itself in its capacity as noema? (*I*, §88c)

By asking what the essence of the noema is, the essence of the perceived as such, Husserl is asking about the essential features of what appears to us in those acts in which, for example, we recognize the real knight or the real white horse as depicted objects. The question of essence is appropriate. Regardless of who is perceiving the de Sica film, if the subject is in the act of recognizing what is depicted, there are certain essential features of the experience. Apperception of the sensa and of the appearance of the white horse will occur, a reaching out to a real object existing independently of the motion picture will occur, and so forth. Of course, a film editor might attend to the manner of cutting in the final sequence of *Shoeshine* (an ordinary cinemagoer may do so, too). The film editor might notice the sensa associated with editing the sequence, for example, in determining whether there are matches or mismatches. But focusing on the editing of a film is not the act of recognizing what the film depicts; it has nothing to do with what the phenomenological analysis is seeking to explain, that is, those acts in which what is depicted, portrayed, and/or symbolized is apprehended.

Husserl concludes the apple tree illustration with reference to the noematic aspect of the experience:

We will await the reply to our question as we wait, in pure surrender, on what is essentially given. We can then describe "that which appears as such," faithfully and in the light of perfect self-evidence. As just one other expression for this we have, "the describing of perception in its noematic aspect." (*I*, §88c)

By bracketing, we are able to look within the relation of subject and object in the moments constituting the perceptual act. We now realize what we could not notice as we were in the midst of the perceptual act. Though we did not realize that we were doing it, we were in fact *codetermining* an appearance, a noema, for example, an appearance of the white horse in our experience of the de Sica film. We did not realize that we were passing through the appearance of the white horse to grasp the real white horse that is the object depicted.

Codetermination of the noemata

With the distinction in mind between *the* object of the perception and the noematic object, the question arises as to what role human subjectivity plays in the perceptual experience. Obviously, if one did not know how engravings represent objects, or if one did not know that knights existed at a particular time in history, one could not apprehend what the engraving represents. The Husserlian account leaves room for *codetermination*[9] of the experience by the perceiver while preserving the distinction between *the* object of the experience and the mediating function of the noemata. Spectators' beliefs, expectations, prior experiences with art objects, knowledge of iconography, and so forth play a determinative role in the nature of the noemata – the perceived object as such. Perceivers of the Dürer would not apprehend the flesh and blood knight as the object depicted were not the experience mediated by the apperception of the appearances of the small figures. Such apperception is founded upon spectatorial contribution; this is very different from saying what idealists say – namely, that the spectator constructs the objects of his or her experience.[10]

Some illustrations may prove helpful in understanding how the perceiver codetermines the noemata but does not constitute the properties of *the* object of perception. Suppose a friend of mine and yours, Claire, has been horribly disfigured in a fire. One day when we both meet her after the tragedy, neither of us is aware of the tragedy that has befallen her, neither of us is aware that it is Claire that we see before us; she is too embarrassed by what has happened and how she now looks to tell us what has happened and that it is she.

As we look at her, we who know Claire from somewhat different circumstances, have a sense that we know this person but cannot place her. Perhaps for you there is a familiar gesture and a certain gait as she walks. Perhaps for me there is a certain look in her eyes that sets off reverberations in me. As each of us struggles to grasp who it is, we engage in the process of recognition somewhat differently. You continue to watch how she walks and gestures; I am attentive primarily to the look in her eyes. Each of us must perform the difficult task of putting aside the characteristic shape and texture of her face, the look of her hair, and we have to put aside the hideous disfigurement.

What each of us succeeds in grasping is that *the* object of our perception, the person we perceive, is Claire. We have done so through the mediation of the noemata. Though we codetermine somewhat different noemata, the object of our perception, Claire, remains unaffected by our activity to grasp who it is we see. She is Claire quite independently of our activity. Whatever characteristics she has obtain quite without regard for our acts of recognizing who it is we see. Nevertheless, our subjectivity plays a role in our acts of recognizing Claire. Had you not frequently seen her walk and gesture before a class, you would not codetermine the mediating noemata the way you do. Had I not had that brief love affair with Claire, I would not be so sensitized by the look in her eyes.

Meanwhile, each of us is bombarded with sensa, "hyletic data." These sensa codetermine the mediating noemata as well. These noemata, which are codetermined by the apperception of the hyletic data and/or subjective activity, are not noticed in the process of grasping who it is that we are looking at; for this reason, they are best described as apperceived. These noemata register on our consciousness; if we perform the reduction, we can become aware of our codetermining activity in constructing them.

In a similar way, you and I experience the Dürer engraving for the first time. We both discover rather readily that a knight (and death and the devil) are depicted. In our discovery process, you may have much more knowledge about the iconographic tradition in which Dürer works while I am relatively ignorant of it. We are bombarded by more or less the same hyletic data. The noemata that mediate your grasp of the knight as the depicted object will no doubt be codetermined differently from those that mediate my recognition. I may not be able to recognize that death is depicted whereas you, with your knowledge of the symbolism utilized in the period, can do so. If, on the other hand, neither of us had ever experienced an engraving before or any art at all, and knew nothing of the institution of knighthood, we would not be able to recognize what is represented.

You the historian and I the film scholar similarly codetermine the mediating appearances, the noemata, differently in the act of recognizing that late-1940s Italian society is portrayed by the de Sica film. Both of us know how motion pictures represent objects, unlike the Australian bushman who has never seen a picture and would not know what to make of what he sees were he to be taken into one of those urban shelters we call a movie theater. However, there are differences between us that show up in how we will codetermine noemata. You know Italian history very well; my knowledge of Italian history is far less in scope than yours. You know little of the history of Italian neorealism; I am a scholar of the movement. You were an American occupation soldier in postwar Italy; I have never been there. You have only a layman's knowledge of Western art history; I am a passionate reader of the history of Western art. You are a 65-year-old man; I am a 30-year-old woman.

As a result of these differences, how things will appear to us, how the appearances will be formed, how the noemata will be codetermined by our activity, will differ. Nevertheless, the important relationship is that, however the noemata are formed, they must succeed in guiding your perception and my perception to the flesh and blood reality of postwar Italian society. The important thing is *not* that we be guided to each of our *concepts* of postwar Italian society, as the idealist would have it. Different noemata can both succeed in guiding perception to postwar Italian society as it was in itself. It is possible to so codetermine the appearances, the noemata, that you will not be able to be guided to the portrayal object. You may be led, by the bombardment of hyletic data, to trigger off thoughts of your experience as an occupation soldier, thereby being led away, by the noemata that get constituted, from the portrayal object, for example, to think of an affair you had then and there. But if you attend to what appears to you with the effort to reach beyond to what is pointed to, it matters not that what appears to me differs from what appears to you. The differences are due to our differing codeterminative activity.

Horizon

Another element in the Husserlian system needs to be added in order to understand the nature of representation, namely, his concept of horizon.[11] The concept of horizon is related to the codetermination of noemata by the activity of consciousness.

Husserl explains how the act of apprehending an object presupposes certain important features of the perceiver's system of background beliefs about relevant features of the object. In the *Cartesian Meditations* he uses the example of looking at dice to illustrate. His aim is to explain how our acts of perception have horizons that are predelineated due to the codeterminative activity of the perceiver:

> The horizons are 'predelineated' potentialities. . . . The predelineation itself, to be sure, is at all time imperfect yet, with its indeterminateness, it has a *structure of determinateness*. For example: the die leaves open a great variety of things pertaining to the unseen faces: yet it is already "construed" in advance as a die, in particular as colored, rough, and the like, though each of these determinations always leaves further particulars open. This leaving open . . . is precisely what makes up the "horizon." (*CM*, 45)

An act of seeing a die, therefore, presupposes the perceiver's system of general background beliefs about die. These beliefs play an essential role in the predelineation of an act's horizon. They prescribe what would and what would not count, for the perceiver, as further determinations of the object as it is given in the present act, that is, features of the object as it appears in our experience (i.e., as noemata), the appearances that mediate our apprehension of the die.

Just as in the case of die in a gambling game, our perception of objects in film is always incomplete ("indeterminate" is the term Husserl uses). When we perceive an Italian boy in the experience of *Shoeshine*, Husserl's insight is that we perceive the whole person, the boy in his fullness, as the object of our perception even though some of him may be unseen. Underlying the seeming paradox of Husserl's view is a crucial contribution that Husserl has made to epistemology.

Perception of any object within or outside a motion picture cannot involve everything about an object; yet the object itself, with all of its properties, whether it be an Italian boy or a white horse or Italian society, is what we perceive. In any view of an Italian boy in *Shoeshine*, for instance, there is an incompleteness. If we see him from in front, his back is unseen. If at another time we see his back, then we do not see his front. If we sense his inner life at a particular time in the film experience (e.g., his intentions to escape from the jail when the fire breaks out at the movie within the movie), we do not sense his dispositions to behave in other circumstances (e.g., whether he would be disposed to attempt escape in less chaotic circumstances). Yet, despite these gaps in our seeing of the boy, we are throughout the film perceiving the boy, with all of his properties.

Idealist analysis contends that the presence of the gaps in our experience of the Italian boy need to be filled in by the constructive activity of the spectator, that we only experience fragments from which personhood can only be spectator constituted. Husserl is telling us, to the contrary, that there are horizons that govern *discovery* of *the* object of our perception (e.g., the Italian boys in *Shoeshine*). In making our contribution to the codetermination of what appears to us, to the noemata, our act of perception is governed in part by horizons, which were acquired in our prior interaction with persons. Horizons are not subjective concepts, varying from person to person, but are intersubjectively valid; horizons have to do with the properties persons actually have, not just properties perceivers at a certain place attribute to them because of their culturally bound conceptual frameworks. In *Experience and Judgment,* Husserl writes:

The object is present from the very first with a character of familiarity; it is already apprehended as an object of a type more or less vaguely determined and already, in some way, known. In this way the direction of the expectations of what closer inspection will reveal in the way of properties is predelineated. (*EJ*, §24a)

We do not start with mere fragmentary sighting of what may or may not be a person and/or Italian boy in the experience of *Shoeshine*. Rather, we start already knowing what properties an Italian boy has. As Husserl puts it, the expectations we have about what the object is, that it is an Italian boy, is "predelineated." Horizons guide us toward the object present before us, the Italian boy. They do *not* guide us to put the *construction* on what appears to us to be an Italian boy. Husserl is speaking directly to the opposing idealist position in these two quotes. We are experiencing an Italian boy, fully and unqualifiedly, with all his properties though not all of his properties are appearing in the experience. We are discovering him, not constructing him out of the sensa. The experience is not to be described as momentary. An object that lasts through time, the Italian boy, is *the* object of our perception. Horizons, which we have acquired from prior experience with persons, guide us in a way that arises at the very same moment as we perceive the boy.

The manner in which these beliefs place further and more specific *constraints* on an act's horizon is explained by Husserl in the following passage from *Experience and Judgment:*

The factual world of experience is experienced as trees, bushes, animals, snakes, birds; specifically as pine, linden, lilac, dog, viper, swallow, sparrow, and so on.... What is given in experience as a new individual is first known in terms of what has been genuinely perceived; it calls to mind the like (the similar). But what is apprehended according to type also has a horizon of possible experience with corresponding predelineations due to familiarity and has, therefore, types of attributes not yet experienced but expected. When we see a dog, we immediately anticipate its additional modes of behavior: its typical way of eating, playing, running, jumping, and so on. We do not actually see its teeth; but although we have never before seen this dog, we know in advance how its teeth will look – not in their individual determination but according to type, inasmuch as we have already had previous and frequent experience of "similar" animals, of "dogs," that they have such things as "teeth," and actual experience may or may not confirm it. (*EJ*, §83a)

The perceiver's beliefs about that particular object, for example, what she or he remembers about it, serve to *constrain* perception of that object. A horizon of the past thus partly governs our perception of objects in the present. On this point Husserl says the following:

No apprehension is merely momentary and ephemeral...the object is pregiven with a new content of sense, it is present to consciousness with the horizon... of acquired cognitions. (*EJ*, §25)

In experiencing *Shoeshine*, our perception of the Italian boys is not given as momentary but is in a way filled out with our knowledge of, and our background beliefs about, Italian life. The horizon of an act includes possible perceptions that can also disappoint rather than fulfill our expectations about the object. If the conflict between background beliefs and current perception is so great, then Husserl speaks of the intended object being "cancelled" (*I*, §§138, 151; *EJ*, §67a).

Each act is thus related to a horizon of other possible acts the perceiver can perform. In perception, our act intends beyond itself, to other possible perceptions the experience of which would characterize the object more closely or in further respects than is the case in our act. The horizon of the object as it is intended comprises the possibilities left open, that is, the set of possible perceptions that would, if they occurred, complete perceptual determinations of the object.

Husserl urges the perspective that there is a frame of indetermination setting limits on the possible acts allowed into the act's horizon. An act's horizon is never completely grasped but is implicit in the act of intending its object. Husserl describes this incompleteness feature as follows:

A thing can in principle be given only "in one respect," and that means...incompletely....A thing is necessarily given in mere "ways of appearing"; and necessarily there is thereby a nucleus of "what is actually presented" surrounded through apprehension by a horizon of ungenuine co-giveness and more or less vague indeterminacy. (*I*, §44)

Husserl then pronounces on this feature of incompleteness:

To remain forever incomplete...is an ineradicable essential of the correlation thing and thing perception. (*I*, §44)

Husserl connects this feature of incompleteness with the horizon governing perception as follows:

Every experience has an experience "horizon."...For example, there belongs to every external perception its reference from the "genuinely perceived" sides of the object of perception to the "co-intended" sides – not yet perceived, but only anticipated....Furthermore, the perception has horizons made up of other possibilities of perception, as perceptions that we could have, if we actively directed the course of perception otherwise: if, for example, we turned our eyes that way instead of this, or if we were to step forward or to one side, and so forth. (*CM*, §19)

As we experience *Shoeshine*, we intend the Italian boys in a way governed by the set of possible appearances that would complete a recognition of Italian boys. That no boy is ever *completely* experienced in a motion picture or in any life experience does not alter the fact that our perception of the boys is guided by the set of possible determinations of Italian boyhood.

The concept of the noema

From the foregoing explanation of Husserl's theory, it should be apparent that the concept of the noema is vital to theorizing about representation. In respect to this centrality for the noema, this section will be devoted to clarifying this concept as well as marshaling textual evidence and systematic considerations to justify the assumption made herein that Husserl was developing a realist account of the noema.

Though Husserl's concept of the noema is responsive to the entire history of epistemogy from Plato onward, it must have been his belief that his conceptualization of the noema was unique. We find him reaching back to the Greek language for the term 'noema' to designate what he wanted the noema to be instead of using existing ordinary language or philosophical language. He was concerned that terms such as 'appearance,' 'meaning,' and 'sense,' had become so encrusted with associations that would obtrude upon an understanding of the knowing process that a neutral term must be found. His view was not Plato's, Aristotle's, Kant's, Frege's, or anyone else's. It nevertheless remains that, in order to explain what Husserl meant by the key term 'the noema,' it is necessary to use existing ordinary and philosophical language. In engaging in this process of explaining what the noema is, it turns out that 'appearance' in a quite heavily qualified sense comes closest to capturing the concept Husserl developed.*

In *Logical Investigations,* the relationship between the act of knowing and its intentional content, on the one hand, and its independently existing object, on the other hand, was left to be a "magical" process. In *Ideas* Husserl introduced the concept of the noema and associated concepts (*Irreell, Abschattung, Erscheinung,* etc.) in an effort to fully account for the relationship. In what follows, attention will be primarily focused, therefore, upon *Ideas,* but, where relevant, passages from *Logical Investigations* will provide a source for understanding as well.

Any adequate account of the noema must explain its place in the network of other concepts in Husserl's system, including the following:

Phenomenon (*Phänomen*)

Appearance, appearing (*Erscheinung*)

Seeming (*Scheinen, erscheinen*)

Perspectival variation (*Abschattung*)

Representation (*Vorstellung, Repräsentation*)

Presentation (*Vorstellung, Präsentation*)

Intention (*Vermeinung, Meinung, Intention*)

Apprehension (*Auffassung*)

Apperception (*Apperception*)

Interpretation (*Deutung*)

Experience (*Erlebnis*)

Perception (*Wahrnehmung*)

Imagination, fancy, phantasy (*Phantasie*).

We shall start the exposition with phenomenon, appearing, and seeming.

In stating the connection of the noema with appearance, this term 'appearance' with all of its associations with matters foreign to Husserl's epistemological project, especially with idealism, must be disentangled and stated in just the sense that will be useful for understanding the noema. Husserl related the noema to appearance in many passages where it seemed that he both needed to include a cer-

---

* If Husserl meant by 'noema' an appearance of what was variously called 'comprehension' by the Port-Royal Logicians or 'connotation' by John Stuart Mill or 'intension' by Sir William Hamilton, he would have said so. David Woodruff Smith and Ronald McIntyre[1] utilize post-Carnapean theory of intension with respect to an opposing interpretation to conceptually map noema. Here, as we have seen, I argue that a notion of appearance, richer than any one in ordinary language and in philosophical language of Husserl's time, constitutes the meaning of 'noema.'

tain concept of appearance and needed to exclude unwanted meanings of appearance.

Martin Heidegger has developed a taxonomy of the meanings of appearance that may be utilized in laying the groundwork for disentangling the various notions of appearance one from another. Heidegger starts with the terms 'phenomenon' and 'appearance.' He reminds us that for the Greeks 'phenomenon' meant to show oneself, to become manifest: "An entity can show itself...in many ways, depending in each case on the kind of access we have to it."[2] Thus, Heidegger is working with the conceptualization that it is the *object* that the perceiver is experiencing; the object is 'appearing' in the sense of showing itself. There is no built-in notion here, as in some well-known uses of 'appearance,' where the appearances are to be distinguished from the reality.[3] Using the Dürer illustration to explain the conceptual map of appearance that Heidegger is developing, one may say that the object represented by the Dürer engraving, the flesh and blood knight, is showing itself in a certain way; it is appearing to perceivers in certain ways.

Heidegger qualifies that the ways in which the object of perception appears depends on our access to it. Our only access in the Dürer case is through vision; in everyday life, our access to the knight would be much more extensive: We could also hear him, touch him, talk with the him, shift our perspective on him, and so forth.

Heidegger notes that an object can appear to us in ways it is not: "An entity can show itself as something which in itself it is *not*."[4] A knight could, for instance, appear as a monk if appropriate religious dress were donned instead of that manner of dress, emblems, and so forth typifying knightly bearing. Heidegger does not have in mind a case where, for example, atmospherics give a misleading appearance – where, for instance, the light accidentally casts shadows over the knight so as to obliterate identifying marks of his knightly status: "Only when the meaning of something is such that it makes a pretension of showing itself...can it show itself as it is not."

In his analysis, Heidegger is distinguishing between 'phenomenon' and 'appearance.' Phenomenon signifies that which shows itself in itself, the manifest. When an object shows itself as it is not, it is appropriate to say: "It looks like something or other; this kind of showing itself is what we call seeming." Thus, the person seems like a monk but is a knight. Semblance is also being distinguished by Heidegger from phenomenon. Heidegger explains that both phenomenon and semblance are to be distinguished from appearance and mere appearance.

In explaining appearance as opposed to phenomenon and semblance, Heidegger starts with symptoms. In speaking of symptoms of a disease, one is thinking of the body as showing itself in ways that indicate conditions that do not show themselves. It is not the infection but the high temperature, a symptom of the infection, that is being shown. Of these cases, Heidegger says:[5]

Thus, appearance, as appearance of "something," does *not* mean showing itself; it means rather the announcing itself by something which does not show itself. Appearing is a *not-showing-itself.*

He continues by distinguishing appearance from semblance:

But the "not" we find here is by no means to be confused with the privative "not" which we used in defining ... semblance.

Heidegger then delineates a central aspect of appearance:

What appears does *not* show itself; and anything which thus fails to show itself, is also something which can never seem.

In the medical example, it is in the nature of some diseases that they do not show themselves. Heidegger is making also the further point that, since seeming to be something requires that the object must announce itself, appearing in this sense would never be "seeming" to be something. If a certain disease appears only in symptoms, then it cannot seem to be some other disease. Symptoms, of course, can be misread so that we may say on some occasions that it seemed that the patient had one disease but really had another. We would not, however, say that the disease AIDS appeared seeming to be cancer.

Heidegger's taxonomy of phenomenon, appearance, and seeming starts to take shape. In order to explain the relationships holding between these concepts, we need other terms that designate the central relationships. Appearance and phenomenon are different in certain ways but are also alike in other ways. Showing (*Zeigen*), announcing (*Melden*), and bringing forth (*Hervorbringen*) have to do with the respects in which phenomenon and appearance are alike and different. Here is how the various cases may be grouped according to the Heideggerian schema:

1. An object shows itself.
2. An object shows itself through something else (e.g., a disease shows itself through symptoms).
3. An object announces itself in and through something else (e.g., a triangle announces itself through a triangular shape).
4. An object brings forth a mere appearance when its real nature cannot be made manifest.

One needs all four of these cases in order to understand the workings of appearance, but case 3 is central.[6]

Case 3 for Heidegger is the proper sense of what appearance is. As he says "appearing is an announcing-itself through something that shows itself."[7] Case 4 is mere appearance. Case 2 is the primordial sense of phenomenon but is intimately bound up with case 1. Heidegger emphasizes that appearing "is never a showing itself in the sense of phenomenon." This is so because appearing is possible only where something is showing itself. Appearing is, therefore, dependent on phenomenon obtaining. This dependency relation, however, does not change the fact that phenomenon and appearing are not the same: "But this showing-itself, which helps make possible the appearing, is not the appearing itself."

In the Dürer case, the depicted knight shows himself *by* appearing in a certain way. Small gray figures appear to us. Heidegger points out that appearance may be used in two senses, senses that must be kept distinct: that which announces itself but does not show itself and that which *does* the announcing (*BT*, 54). In the Dürer illustration, the former would be the real knight, the latter would be the small gray figures.

A core connection between the noema and appearance consists in the concept that the only way to seek the reality of the object is through the ways the object appears to perceivers. The case 3 appearance take several forms, that is, an object may announce itself in and through something else in a variety of ways including the relations of seeming and mere appearance. For instance, that the railroad tracks appear to converge in the distance is a mere appearance. At that distance in actuality they remain as far apart as in our foreground. But being a mere appearance does not make the appearance useless for knowledge. Quite the contrary, the appearance of the tracks coming together in the distance is a part of a law-governed system of presentations for knowing the objects for what they are, according to Husserl. Appearances function according to a system involving self-correction. For Husserl, "for the phenomenology of 'true reality,' the phenomenology of 'empty illusion' is wholly indispensable" (*I*, §151,388). As Dallas Willard expresses Husserl's views on the role of appearances in knowledge:

Appearances are deceiving only if the lines of inquiry which they themselves determine are not adequately followed up on. In a sense, they are *always* profoundly truthful. . . . We cannot cognitively approach any object except through its appearances; but its appearances, when systematically pursued in accordance with their own nature, will *always* reveal the general essence and existence (or else non-existence) of the respective type of object. That, if we may so speak, is what appearances are for.[8]

In many places Husserl equates the noema with the perceived object as such.[9] In other places, the noema is described as that which is *Irreell*. In explaining further what the noema is, it will be important to indicate the meaning of these two additional concepts and relationships to the various cases of appearance.

Section 97 of *Ideas* is one of the crucial passages that any interpretation of the noema must take into account. In this section, Husserl is exploring the relationship between the noema and a perspectival variation (*Abschattung*), another of the related concepts to appearances. Reading this section with case 3 appearance in mind helps explain Husserl's view.

Husserl begins the section by explaining the ways in which the noematic is nicht-*Reell*. He illustrates his exposition with the case of a simple perception of a tree in the garden (*I*, 260). He gives examples of how the tree appears to us – "at one moment appearing to be motionless, then stirred by the wind." He also gives examples of how our perception of it affects its appearance:

We see this tree there...presenting also modes of appearance which differ greatly in so far as during the course of our continued observation we shift our spatial position in regard to it, stepping to the window maybe, or changing the position of head or eyes, and at the same time perhaps, relaxing the mechanism of accommodation or tightening it up. (*I*, 260)

These appearances are attributed to a variety of real objects considered from the natural standpoint – to the real object as changes to it, to a real relationship of the real object to our real psychophysical subjectivity and to our real subjectivity itself (*I*, 260). Once the reduction has been performed, however, differentiations may be made between what is *Reell* (i.e., an integral part of the experience considered apart from real things) and what is *Irreell* (i.e., *not* an integral part of the purified experience).

Husserl identifies the status of the noema as *Irreell* as follows:

While the "perceived tree as such," or alternately, the full noema which is not affected by the suspending of the reality of the tree itself and of the whole real world, does indeed belong to the essence of the perceptual experience in itself, on the other hand this noema...is as little contained [as] *Reell* in the perception as is the tree of the real natural order. (*I*, 261)

That is, it is neither part nor property of the mental act. Husserl remarks that material and noetic constituents are to be found in the purified experience in contrast with the noematic.

To explicate the noematic factors, Husserl then shifts his illustration from perception of the tree to the color of the tree, under the condition of a transcendental reduction. He says that the color, "as bracketed, belongs to the noema" (*I*, 261), though it is not a *Reell* part of the perceptual experience. He adds, however, that:

We also find in the experience [*Erlebnis*] a color-like something . . . the hyletic-phase of the concrete experience in which the noematic or "objective" color manifests itself in varying perspectives. (*I*, 261)

Husserl remarks that we are aware of this noematic color, that is, the color (case 3) appearance is in itself unchanged though it "runs through its perspective-variations [*Abschattungen*] in a continuous variety of sensory colors." He puts the relationship between the color and the *Abschattungen* as follows:

We see a tree unchanged in color – its own color as a tree – while the position of the eyes, the relative orientations, change in many respects, the glance wanders ceaselessly over the trunk and branches, while we step nearer at the same time and thus in different ways excite the flow of perceptual experience. (*I*, 261)

Husserl contends that that which "exhibits" itself in its variety via *Abschattungen* has its place in the noema (*I*, 262). Husserl then refers to the transcendentally constituted product, shaped on the basis of the material experiences (hyletic data) and through the noetic functions (the giving of an intentional direction to them). This transcendentally constituted product is "indeed something given" and self-evidently so (*I*, 263), but it is *Irreell*. As Husserl puts it:

It belongs to the experience [*Erlebnis*] in a completely different sense from that in which the *Reellen* and consequently proper constituents of the experience belong to it. (*I*, 263)

He then directly marks the *Irreell* status of the noema:

The reference to the phenomenological reduction and similarly to the pure sphere of experience as "transcendental," depends precisely on our finding in this reduction an absolute sphere of materials and noetic forms, to whose interlacings, nicely articulated in accord with an immanent essential necessity, belongs this wonderful conscious possession of something definitely or definably given in such and such a way, standing over against consciousness itself as in principle other, *irreelles*, transcendent. (*I*, 263; italics added)

Husserl then marks the value of recognizing this element within transcendentally purified experience:

Here is the ultimate source for the only conceivable solution of the deepest problems of knowledge affecting the essential nature and the possibility of objectively valid knowledge of the transcendent. (*I*, 263)

It was this element, the noema, that was not part of the explanatory machinery of *Logical Investigations*. He then sketches out the significance of the noema: The noematic is the object residue that is left over after the reduction has occurred; the noematic forms are that in terms of which anything is intended or given, what it is given as (*I*, 264). Husserl reminds us that perception does not consist in just holding *the* object of perception presently before us but that an essential aspect of any perceptual act is to have the object appear to us with a "unity of a certain noematic content" (*I*, 264), which will be different for other perceptions of the same object though always prescribed by relevant horizons (*I*, 264).

In Section 98 of *Ideas*, lest anyone think that the noema is something other than an object we apperceive, though not *the* object of the perception, he says, upon bracketing, we can direct our glance upon the experience and its *reell* or "in the contrary direction upon the noema e.g., the seen tree as such. Now what is given through this latter glance is indeed itself, logically speaking, an object" (*I*, 264).

He then describes the nature of this noematic object; it is "one that is wholly dependent. Its *esse* consists exclusively in its *percipi*...the *percipi* does not contain the *esse* as *reelles* constituent" (*I*, 264).

Husserl distances himself from Berkeley's doctrines of *esse est percipi* as follows:

Its *esse* consists exclusively in its "percipi," except that the meaning of this statement is about as far removed as it can be from that of Berkeley. (*I*, 265)

Since in the context of transcendentally reduced perception, if not *Reell*, then the noema is *Irreell*.

The distinction between *Reell* and *Irreell* is indispensable for explaining the noema. In *Logical Investigations*, the parallel distinction was between what is *Reellen* and the intentional content of an act:

By the real...content of an act we mean the sum total of its concrete and abstract parts, in other words, the sum total of the partial experience that really constitute it. (*LI*, §16, 576)

The *Irreell*, or intentional content of an act, is recognizable once one has shifted "from our natural-scientific, psychological standpoint to an ideal-scientific, phenomenological [standpoint]" (*LI*, §16, 577). In so bracketing, Husserl says:

We thus achieve insights in a pure phenomonology which is here oriented, whose descriptions are in every way "ideal" and free from experience i.e., from presuppositions of real existence. (*LT*, §16, 577)

In the interpretation of the noema developed here, a concept of apperception has played a crucial role. Husserl's reviews of other philosopher's work in the 1890s and his two great early works *Logical Investigations* and *Ideas* contain many discussions concerned with distinguishing two ways of being aware of objects, one of them involving an object of perception, the other involving passing through what appears to perceivers as a part of the process of perception. *Logical Investigations I*, §23, seems a prime example: The title of the section is "Apperception as connected with expression and with intuitive presentations" (p. 309). In the section, Husserl speaks of two ways in which objects are registered in consciousness. He uses "lived through" to designate the perceivers' relation to sensations, that is, perceivers live through sensations (*LI*, 309). Husserl clarifies that he does not mean to imply that:

Consciousness first looks at its sensations, then turns them into perceptual objects, and then bases an interpretation on them, which is what really happens when we are objectively conscious of physical objects e.g., sounded words.... Sensations plainly only become presented objects in psychological reflection... the perceived *object* appears, while the sensational complex is as little perceived as is the act in which the perceived object is as such constituted. (*LI*, 310)

Husserl elaborates on these two kinds of awareness:

Phenomenological analysis teaches us, further, that sense-contents provide, as it were, the analogical building stuff for the content of the object presented by their means. Hence, talk of colors, extensions, intensities, etc., as, on the one hand, sensed, and as, on the other hand, perceived or imagined. (*LI*, 310)

In the 1890s Husserl was using the term *Repräsentation* (with the *ae* spelling) to bring out the notion of two different ways of being aware, believing apparently that there were too many unfortunate associations with *representation* (spelled with an *e*) to make it feasible to use the term in bringing out this distinction.

For example, in a critical review of H. Cornelius's *Versuch einer Theorie der Existentialurteile*,[10] Husserl speaks of the process of apprehension in which an individual utilizes what is lived through to represent an object. Husserl complains that Cornelius reduces all judgments to mere noticing while denying the distinction of two psychic functions *within* perception.[11] Husserl continues by making a distinction between phantasm and corresponding perceptual content and how we live through it (*H*, 375). He then proceeds with a discussion of Repräsentation in contrast to mere noticing:

The Repräsentation is, in contrast to mere noticing, a fundamentally different "mode of being conscious of a content," and indeed precisely that mode which stamps the content as a repraesentant of an object, which object itself is no part, no fragment, and also no non-independent moment, of the "representing" act but rather resides in it only "intentionally." (H, 376)

Then Husserl speaks of intuitionalizing phantasma and the need not to confuse the comparison of phantasma with that of the objects represented by means of them (49) (H, 377).

From the preceding systematic considerations and textual evidence, the noema may be best understood in terms of a realist epistomology. It is an appearance[12] in the heavily qualified sense explained herein. In the experience of the Dürer engraving, it is apperceived as part of the process of apprehending the real knight. In performing the reduction, the noema may be recognized to have the status of being *Irreell*. The noema is codetermined by the act of consciousness in contradistinction to *the* object of perception, which exists independently of the acts of the knowing mind.

The ontology of cinematic representation

With central elements of Husserl's conceptual framework in hand as well as a sense of how phenomenology would apply to the analysis of artistic and cinematic representation, attention may now be turned to the ontological and epistemological grounds for a phenomenological account of cinematic representation as opposed to that of contemporary film theory, which has been nominalist and idealist.

The nominalist undergrowth of contemporary film theory may be seen to be an unsatisfactory ground for its effort to give an account of cinematic representation. It should become apparent that a realist grounding provides a much more plausible basis upon which to analyze depiction, portrayal, and symbolism in cinema.

Nominalism (in the sense used here) is the view that only individual things exist.[1] In the case of film, nominalism would hold that only images and sound exist in film experience. In the long history of nominalism, a diametrically opposed view has been that of realism (in one of its senses). Realism is the position that in addition to individuals there also are universals that become exemplified in individuals. With respect to film, realism would hold that critics apprehend what a motion picture represents by means of identifying universals that indwell within the individual things in our film experience.

In Kurosawa's *The Seven Samurai* (*Shichinin no samurai*) it may seem that we experience a narrative: Bandits terrorize a village, samurai are hired to defend the village, battle ensues, samurai and villagers win out. For contemporary theory, with its nominalist underpinnings, the contention is that there are really only images and sounds in our experience – what we have been calling hyletic data or sensa – a figure rides screen left, large shape in the foreground, a high-pitched sound, and so forth.

For realism, in addition to such individual things existing, there are also universals exemplified. In apprehending what *The Seven Samurai* depicts, critics utilize universals such as man, farmer, bandit, samurai, sword, fight, selection, space, time, and so forth to recognize the objects, events, and persons depicted. These universals are exemplified in the individual things we experience in the Kurosawa film. We see a figure ride across the screen moving screen left. We also find the universal spaceness exemplified there as well.

The nominalist undergrowth of contemporary film theory

Under the influence of movements within contemporary film theory, primarily theories of enunciation and spectatorship promoted by Roland Barthes and cinesemiotics formulated and developed by Christian Metz, a long-standing vocabulary for representation has been problematized. We shall see that a conceptual framework with a long and problematic history behind it, nominalism, provides the grounds. It had seemed natural to attribute representation to motion pictures with real or fictional objects as referents.

1. Murnau depicts a vampire in *Nosferatu* (*Eine Symphonie des Grauens*).
2. Murnau and Herzog portray their vampire figures rather differently in their respective versions of *Nosferatu* (subtitled *Eine Symphonie des Grauens* and *Phantom der Nacht*).
3. Herzog symbolizes the evil persisting in the German soul via his portrayal of the vampire.

For a variety of reasons (to be explained later), a major rethinking of representation has taken place due to the attractiveness of nominalist theory with the result that, as we shall shortly see, only arbitrary grounds for ascriptions of representation are posited. Instead of there being independently existing real and fictional objects, persons, events and states of affairs represented by motion pictures, contemporary film theory regards representations as constructions of spectator imaginative activity governed by prevailing cultural and cinematic codes.

With the coming to prominence of contemporary film theory, deeply embedded assumptions about representation become problematic, especially ascriptions of realism in cinema. Whereas previously it had been thought that there are two concepts of realism, one stylistic and the other epistemological, there now is thought to be only one concept, an arbitrarily constructed one at that. Before, epistemological realism in representation meant that a type of entity (e.g., a man) was depicted or an individual (e.g., Kikuchiyo, the warrior played by Toshiro Mifune in *The Seven Samurai*) was portrayed, while stylistic realism referred to the passing fashions in the arts (e.g., "the realism of the post-war Japanese cinema gave way to a counterrealism in the Japanese new wave"). Now, all attributions of realism are thought arbitrary, merely markings of our habits in organizing the images we experience in a film; in no way is there such a thing as realistically depicting a man or realistically portraying a particular warrior.

This reduction of realism in cinematic representation to a purely stylistic notion, which we could call the elimination of realistic representation, will be the focus here. In advancing the presiding, highly relativistic conception of cinematic representation, an ancient conceptual framework, nominalism, has been enlisted by contemporary film theory.

In the case of film critics' attribution of realistic representation, the governing nominalist concept is as follows: There exists a group of individual things – images and sounds – that are the only things that are really present in the critics' phenomenal fields as they, the critics, experience a film. These images are given to critics with no connections between these images/sounds; accordingly they exemplify no universals. Of course, critics make connections among the images/sounds, but these connections are derived via cultural and cinematic codes.

For instance, it may have seemed that a host of films have been ordered via narrative, that is, it may have seemed that events were taking place before our eyes with beginnings, middles, and ends, with characters undertaking actions, and so forth. *The Seven Samurai* begins with bandit attacks on a village; there is a middle where samurai and villagers unite together against the bandits; there is an end where the farmers have returned to their fields. However, according to contemporary theory, there are only images/sounds before us that admit of many possible orderings; narrative ordering is only one of many orderings, all equally arbitrary. To give priority to narrative or to think that events are being portrayed on the screen is to radically misunderstand what is really there, which is just a series of images and sounds.

Nominalism underlies this contemporary theoretical view. It is not surprising that a leading twentieth-century advocate of nominalism, Nelson Goodman,[2] is often cited by film theorists for having provided the theoretical justification for the contemporary approach to cinematic representation.

J. Dudley Andrew, in explaining contemporary film theory's idea of representation, describes how "Goodman has pursued...a pluralistic and Nominalist philosophy which makes explicit use of art."[3] In connecting Goodman's nominalism with representation, Andrew remarks: "There is no primary real world which we subsequently subject to various types of representation (Goodman) contends. Rather it makes far more sense to speak of multiple worlds which individuals construct." Andrew continues by explaining that cinema represents some object not "against some supposed 'reality' existing beyond representation" but rather in terms of some particular system of representation or other with none having any inherent priority over any other. Realism simply becomes that manner of representation that seems most natural to us at a particular time or place not what corresponds with how things are.[4]

Goodman argues for his view as follows: "I have argued that the world is as many ways as it can truly be described, seen, pictured, etc., and there is no such thing as the way the world is."[5] The "touchstone of Realism" as Goodman calls it has its locus in

Practice [having] rendered the symbols so transparent that we are not aware of any effort, of any alternatives or of making any interpretation at all. ... Realism is relative: determined by the system of representation standard for a given time.[6]

Goodman elaborates as follows:

To make a faithful picture, come as close as possible to copying the object just as it is. This simple-minded injunction baffles me; for the object before me is a man, a swarm of atoms, a complex of cells, a fiddler. ... If all are ways the object is, then none is *the way* the object is. ... I have argued that the world is as many ways as it can be truly described, seen, pictured, etc., and there is no such things as *the way* the world is.[7]

Søren Kjørup, in developing a theory of cinematic representation inspired by Goodman, argues that representation obtains via codes; this is so, he contends, because visual reality is itself coded:

This is exactly what my claim is. Visual reality is coded, although not necessarily in the sense that human beings organize things according to rules to make them convey certain messages or express certain feelings. Rather it is coded in the sense that we interpret certain features of the visual as signs.[8]

Kjørup gives the following as an example:

Seeing that a man is a man by his mustache and that he is rather old by his gray hair is interpreting the film just as one would interpret visual reality. ... A person who is characterized as having gray hair and mustache is by these very features further characterized as a man and as rather old. This must mean that a further rule that belongs to a whole code of visual appearances makes a certain visual appearance mean something.

. . .

Visual reality is coded not in the sense that a linguistic system has been constructed, using as syntactical elements things like age, sex, and social status, but rather in the sense that people do in actuality interpret these things in these ways and that such interpretations seem to be based on systems of the kinds indicated.[9]

Andrew explains further the connection of the nominalist framework with semiotics in commenting that "the semiotic work of such theorists as [Christian] Metz and [Roland] Barthes has disclosed the cleverness of the realist system [providing] an impetus for both critics and filmmaker to go beyond realism."[10] This is so because, as Andrew puts it: "Realism in the cinema is driven by a desire to make the audience ignore the process of signification and to grasp directly the film's plot or intrigue."[11] Andrew then explains how Roland Barthes

suggests a method whereby narrative can be treated as a practice, conventional, and even rhetorical in which fragments are joined in a way to promote an illusionistic experience.... Roland Barthes is the prophet of the artistic texts urging us to escape the trap of narrative, a trap that naturalizes conventions.... He lobbies for a free interchange between codes, instead of the dominance of one of them, narrative.[12]

For Barthes, as Andrew notes, criticism is part of the object it seeks to explain with each reading of the text having the potential to produce a new meaning.[13]

The nominalist problematic

In assessing the respective ontological frameworks for contemporary film theory and for phenomenology in accounting for cinematic representation, two general considerations are relevant:

1. The nominalist provides a false picture of the perceptual situation involved in apprehending cinematic representation.
2. Nominalism has difficulty in accounting for the critical communication utilized in describing and analyzing cinematic representation.

We shall look at each of these considerations in detail.

First, the description of the perceptual situation of film viewing that issues from the underlying nominalist framework distorts the process that actually takes place in film experience. Phenomenology reveals the distortions while indicating a more proper direction for our conceptualization of the film experience. The notion that what is really before us is simply a series of images/sounds is false to film experience. It is a highly artificial abstraction of the concrete experience we have of a film. There is no reason to suppose that the object of our perception of a film is merely a series of images and sounds. To be sure, for film editors seated before their editing table, it may *seem* that their work is accomplished with merely a series of images and sounds. However, for film spectators (including critics), the film experience is something very different than a series of images and sounds that may be ordered in an indefinite number of ways.

As we have seen, in Husserlian language, consciousness admits of intentionality. By the intentionality of consciousness, Husserl means to mark the fact that consciousness is always consciousness of something. The perceptual situation is conceived as one in which perceivers grasp the objects of their experience, an object that transcends their cognitive acts. The experience of film involves such a transcendence wherein the mind cognitively grasps objects that neither are nor can be parts or properties of mental acts. Moreover, in *transcendence*, the objects reached out to (in their existence) are indifferent to mental acts involved in their apprehension; accordingly, they exist, in an important way, in themselves.

For instance, the objects of spectator/critical perception in an experience of Kurosawa's *The Seven Samurai* are not a series of images/sounds, for example, a shot of a figure riding across screen space left, a high pitched cry, and so forth, or more abstractly not merely patterns of light and shadows, some faint, some vivid. Instead, the objects of perception are persons, things, events, actions, and states of affairs. There is, for instance, early on in the film the action of finding a group of samurai to defend a besieged village against marauding bandits. It is this complex action that spectators "intend," that is the object of their mental act of perceiving in this early part of *The Seven Samurai*. This action is not part of the spectators' mental acts of perception. As such, it transcends their mental acts although the spectators' perceptions grasp it.

In ontology, evidence in the strict sense cannot be given to support either realism or nominalism. The greater efficacy of the realist account over that of the nominalist has its locus in a far more plausible description of perceptual experience. Only by looking into one's experience to see whether or not sensa are the objects of perception or are only apperceived can one decide the issue. There seems to be every reason, upon such examination of one's experience, to find the realist theory the most compelling.

As with any complex action, there is contained within the larger action many smaller actions – interviewing available samurai, testing the ability of interviewees, observing a fight involving a potential samurai selectee, and so forth. In the course of grasping any one of the smaller actions, say, for example, the fight involving the possible samurai selectee, the spectators undergo the experience of being exposed to the images/sounds to which the nominalist calls attention. However, these images do not become objects of perception but rather, as analyzed here, are apperceived, passed through, not made the objects of perception. These apperceived hyletic data serve to *guide* perception in the act of grasping *the* object of perception. They are not parts of the object but rather serve to *constrain* the act of perception.

Thus in perceiving the selection of the samurai defenders, spectators undergo experiences in which they apperceive patterns of light and shadow, screen direction relationships, sound textures, and so forth, but their intentional aim is the samurai defender selection. For contemporary film theorists to argue that narrative is but an arbitrary ordering of the images/sounds and that the images/sounds are really the only objects we experience at a film screening involves overlooking the distinction between apperception and perception. Indeed, the aim of perception, the intentional direction of consciousness in a film experience such as that of T*he Seven Samurai,* is a grasping of events with narrative structure in them: Bandits attack, villagers seek assistance from samurai, battle takes place, bandits are driven off. Beginnings, middles, and ends obtain.

Though not all films have narratively structured events as the object of perception, those that do, like *The Seven Samurai,* are not merely *perceived under* the category of narrative by a community of spectators/critics accustomed to ordering their experience in that way. Events are indeed the objects of spectator perception. They are fictional events, to be sure, but events nevertheless with narrative structure as a feature.

In experiencing the Kurosawa film, spectators do not perform the mental abstraction of finding, in their perceptual fields, merely patterns of light and shadow or sensations of screen movement or certain sound textures as they apprehend what the film represents. Though it is true that in our experience there are such patterns and often such movements, it is true but irrelevant to the correct analysis of the mental act of perceiving the film's representations. There are, of course, film experiences, often provided by the independent cinema, in which one does find a pattern of light and shadow or mere screen direction as the objects of perception. Such facts about certain independent films have nothing to do with the experience of a film such as *The Seven Samurai,* which is not structured that way.

Therefore, in contemporary film theory, representation of reality has been conceptualized as the ordering of images and sounds according to what is transparent for a community of appreciators at a particular time and place. Correlatively, the reality of representation is that it is a process involving arbitrarily grounded conventions governing the ordering of the film's images and sounds.

By contrast, for the phenomenological model, representation of reality and the reality of representation in film are assimilated to the pattern of everyday life perception in many ways. Representations in cinema guide spectators' perception of the persons, objects, events, and states of affairs depicted and portrayed by the film. These objects transcend the mental acts employed in perception of them. The individual shots, the images, and sounds of the film are apperceptively experienced not perceived. What is really there in the experience of spectators are not just images and sounds but (e.g., for *The Seven Samurai*) fictional objects and events that sensations, apperceptively registered in consciousness, guide spectator perception to discover.

The mystery that surrounds the success of critical communication on the nominalist model is not to be found on the phenomenological account of representation. The ability to undergo apperception and to be guided by them to transcend the mental act to grasp the object of perception is as natural a capacity as human perceivers possess. As Noel Carroll puts it:

Psychological evidence strongly supports the contention that we learn to recognize what pictures ... stand for as soon as we come to be able to recognize the objects ... that serve as the models for the picture. Picture recognition is not a skill acquired over and above object recognition.... A child raised without pictorial representaions will, after being shown a couple of pictures, be able to identify the referent of any picture of an object of which he or she is familiar. The rapid development of this picture recognition capacity contrasts strongly with the acquisition of a symbol system such as language. Upon mastering a couple of words, the child is nowhere near mastering the entire language.... Very shortly the child just sees what the picture is of; the child doesn't read the picture or decode it or go through some process of inference.[14]

Second, establishing the existence of universals and refuting the nominalist claim that only particulars exist is at the center of the realist theory. In *Logical Investigations II*, Husserl gave many arguments for the existence of universal and against nominalism.[15] We shall look at some of these arguments to have a sense of how Husserl proceeds on these ontological matters; it will have to be left to the reader to pursue all of the detail in *Logical Investigation II*. Once the enormous problems for a nominalist analysis become apparent, a realist grounding for theory of representation may become far more attractive than it has been. A sensitivity to the issues in the debate between nominalist and realist about the existence of universals could be an important first step in moving contemporary film theory away from its unfortunate attachment to a nominalist support for a theory of representation.

To set the stage for understanding Husserl's rejection of nominal-

ism, we may turn to D. M. Armstrong who pinpoints the starting point
for the two ontological positions:

Everybody agrees that particulars have properties ... The piece of paper before
me is a particular. It is white, so it has a property. It rests upon a table, so it
is related to another particular. Such gross facts are not ... in dispute between
Nominalist and Realists. ... We start with a basic agreement, then: that in
some minimal or pre-analytic sense there are things having certain properties
and standing in certain relation.[16]

For both the realist and nominalist, terms such as 'white,' 'black,' 'samurai,' 'bandit,' 'fighting,' apply to particulars. From this original point
of agreement, the two positions immediately diverge with respect to
how to account for these facts:

Nominalists deny that there is any genuine or objective identity in things
which are not identical. ... The fundamental contention of Nominalism is that
all things that exist are only particulars.[17]

By contrast,

Realists hold that "there genuinely is, or can be, something identical in things
which are not identical. Besides particulars, there are universals."[18]

For the nominalist, the term 'samurai' applies to what appears to us
in the Kurosawa film because spectators put the construction samurai,
a relationship among what they see and what they hear, on the individual things in their experience, images and sounds. For the realist,
the term 'samurai' applies because the universal – samurai-ness – is
exemplified in what appears to us as we experience the film.

Armstrong points out that "in the dispute between Realism and
Nominalism, the onus of proof lies with the latter [the nominalist]."[19]
As support for this view, he argues that:

Ordinary thought and discourse recognizes identity both of particulars and of
property, sort and kind. Indeed, without the distinction between sameness of
thing and sameness of property or kind, thought and discourse would be impossible. The terms "token" and "type" are terms of art, but the distinction
which they mark is admitted by everyone. All that the Nominalist can hope to
do is give a reductive analysis ... of types.[20]

For the realist, whiteness would be the type and an instance of a white
thing would be a token.[21]

As mentioned earlier, the nominalist has difficulty explaining how
the complex language of film criticism came about and can be used so
successfully if, as the nominalist theory holds, critics and their read-

ers are always dealing only with individual things with no universals indwelling, no whiteness, no blackness, no samurai-ness, and so forth. The nominalist must reduce statements about types such as whiteness or samurai-ness to statements about arbitrary ways of constructing types out of these not-repeatable individual things. In ordinary life and film critical discourses, a distinction between the type (whiteness) and the token of the type (an instance of white) is deeply embedded. The nominalist must persuade us that there is only what is called the token and what is called types are merely spectator constructions.

Armstrong identifies several major lines of nominalism to defend its view that only particulars exist, that no universals such as whiteness, two-ness, and so forth exist. All nominalist positions must provide an answer to the questions: "How to account for the apparent...identity of numerically distinct particulars? How can two different things both be white or both be on the table?"[22] He points out:

However, although all Nominalists agree that all things that exist are only particulars, they by no means agree about the way that the problem of the apparent identity of nature is to be solved.[23]

Armstrong cautions that

in practice the different types of Nominalism are not very sharply cut off from each other. There is always a tendency for proponents of one variety, particularly under pressure, to pass to another analysis in the course of exposition or argument. The reason for this...is that the Nominalist's real attachment is to the doctrine that whatever exists is only a particular....The particular solution [the nominalist] adopts in order to solve the problem of apparent identity of nature or kind is a matter of secondary concern to the Nominalist.[24]

In *Logical Investigation II,* Husserl's arguments for the existence of universals and his clarification of the nature of universals rest on a distinction between real and ideal.* For Husserl,

the real is the individual with all its parts. It is here and now. Temporality satisfied us as the characteristic mark of reality...all that matters...is the contrast with the non-temporal "being" of the ideal. (*LI,* 351–2)

Universals, by contrast, are ideal. Though they are not part of what is real – they are neither in space nor in time – they nevertheless enter

---

* It was Husserl's view that Immanuel Kant failed to make the distinction between the real and the ideal. "The obscurities in Kant's *Critique of Pure Reason* result from his never having made clear to himself the peculiar character of pure Ideation, the adequate survey of conceptual essences....He accordingly lacked the phenomenologically correct concept of the a priori" (*LI,* 833).

into the act of apprehending the properties of particulars (*LI*, 351–2). He says of ideal objects:

Ideal objects...[as opposed to fictions] truly exist. Evidently there is not merely a good sense in speaking of such objects (e.g., the number 2, of the quality of redness, of the principle of contradiction, etc.) in conceiving them as sustaining predicates. (*LI*, 352f.)

In *The Seven Samurai* case, universals such as whiteness, blackness, samurai-ness, and so forth enter into the apprehension of a depicted event: a fight between samurai and bandits with certain black and white compositional values. They are ideal; hence, they are not part of the real in the experience as are individual instances of black and white. Universals as ideal objects are not spectator constructions but that by means of which spectators identify the properties of the depicted event, the fight.

In order to establish the existence of universals, these ideal objects, Husserl needs to show that some things that have predicates are not individuals. Husserl appeals to the experience we have when we apprehend that something is red. Here is his phenomenology of the experience:

As universal objects differ from singular ones, so too do our acts of apprehending them. We do something wholly different, looking at an intuited concretum, we refer to its sensed redness, the singular aspect existing here and now, and if, on the other hand, we refer to the species Redness, as when we say Redness is a color. And just as, while looking upon some concrete case, we refer, not to it, but to its universal, its Idea, so, while regarding several acts of ideation, we rise to the inwardly evident recognition of the identity of those ideal unities which are meant in our single acts. And it is identity in the authentic, strictest sense, the same species or species of the same genus. (*LI*, 149)

Thus, Husserl is arguing that we find by introspection certain acts to be of a type different than those directed upon individuals, that is, considering some red thing versus recognizing that redness is a color.

To return to the examples of the two versions of *Nosferatu* at the beginning of this chapter, when we consider how Nosferatu is attracted to the blood oozing from Harker's cut finger (in the early dining room scene) in the Murnau original and in the Herzog "remake," we may consider that red is the color of blood in both cases. In leaving our act of apprehending the individual instance of red in either film (though Murnau's film is in black and white we know the blood is red) to focus on our act of apprehending that red is the color of the blood in both films, we may realize that the two acts are different, a realization that undermines a nominalist argument that there are just individual red things. If the nominalist were correct, the acts ought to be the same, which they are not.

Husserl also argues that we can find, immediately recognize, the same element in many different individuals of the same kind. For instance, 2 is a number. If 2 were not to be an ideal object but rather a real thing, it would have to have its locus as a real thing in being some group of two things or events. But 2 cannot be any group because no group is a number:

If we suppose that a group of two individual objects is a number, and let it be completely undetermined as to which group we may mean, then we should also say so; then, in any case, with the saying the thought is changed. (*LI*, 341)

Husserl is saying that if we have in mind two men and we were to say, "This group of two men is a number," we would be directly aware that we do not mean "number" in the same sense we did when we said that 2 is a number. That is, the predicate assigned to the group of men cannot be the one assigned to 2.

Husserl also argues that we can immediately recognize the same element in many different individuals. Redness survives the passing away of many red things and precedes the coming to be of other red things. Husserl aims to show that the nominalist views cannot escape assuming an identity between elements of things that are not identical. I shall illustrate how he argues against nominalism. Husserl focuses in one case on whether or not resemblance can provide the needed unity without falling back on universals in the account. He illustrates with the example of looking at a white piece of paper:

I recognize this paper as paper and as white and thereby make clear to myself the general sense of the expressions "paper" and "white as such," but I need not carry out any intuitions of likeness nor any comparisons. (*LI*, 343–4)

Husserl moreover argues that the nominalist position leads to an infinite regress. Being a member of a class is the target for Husserl as a justification for there existing only particulars:

The conception we are criticizing operates with "circles of similars,"...we must be in a position to say what distinguishes these "circles of similars" among themselves. It is plain that...we cannot avoid in infinitum. An object A is similar to other objects, to one object in the respect a, to another in respect b, etc. But such "respects" do not imply that a species is there, which effects unity. What then unifies the circle of similars determined e.g., by Redness, as against the circle determined by Triangularity?...[The reply says]:

These are differing similarities. If A and B are similar in respect of red and A and C in respect of Triangularity, these similarities are compared, and form genera and species, just as their absolute members do. We should then have to have recourse to similarities, and so on in infinitum. (*LI*, 345)

If an argument can only be generated leading to an infinite regress, the argument is incoherent.

Husserl's contentions against nominalism proceed along familiar lines (most exhaustively treated by Armstrong in his *Nominalism and Realism*) to provide grounds for rejecting nominalism as grounds for one's theories. We have seen that contemporary film theory, explicitly or implicitly, has been relying on nominalism to ground its theories of cinematic representation.* These arguments raise the most serious of objections to views that analyze representation independently of the existence of universals. Universality in things is not an idea in the mind but instantiation of universals in things.

Considering again the vocabulary of cinematic representation, with the distinction in mind between ideal and real, critical communication (the acts involved in critics communicating with their readers) may be quite plausibly comprehended in terms of the realist model. In apprehending that Murnau depicts a vampire or portrays the vampire differently than does Herzog or that Herzog symbolizes something about the German soul as well as communicating these representational relationships to the readers of criticism, critics utilize ideal objects, universals, in accomplishing their grasp of what these motion pictures represent. Although vampireness is not a real thing as Orlock is, it is exemplified in that real object Orlock. It is in apprehending the presence of that universal that critics/appreciators are able to grasp what the Murnau motion picture depicts, a vampire.

The presence of universals indwelling in the real objects in motion pictures extends to hyletic data as well as to the noematic objects and to *the* object of the act of apprehending representation. As Husserl's examples show, the most basic vocabulary that critics use, terms like 'red,' 'space,' 'two,' and so forth depend on the presence of ideal objects, for example, redness, spaceness, twoness. That the highly com-

---

* Christian Metz's cinesemiotics assumes a predicate nominalism as its foundation. "For the Predicate Nominalist, in answer to the question 'in virtue of what do general terms apply?' e.g., a predicate such as 'identical with the planet Venus,' the answer is in virtue of nothing." For Metz the individual things in our experience are best understood as signs. The individual filmmaker's codes, cinematic codes, cultural codes, and so forth serve as the means by which these signs are decoded into types of things represented in the film – in *The Seven Samurai*, white, samurai, bandit, and so forth. By contrast, Nelson Goodman holds a concept nominalism. "Realism is relative ... determined by the system of representation standard for a given time." In neither the predicate nominalist nor in the concept nominalist case is it a matter of how the world is in itself independent of the activities of the knowing mind.[25]

plex and effective critical vocabulary that has evolved in literary and film criticism is quite plausibly accounted for by the assumption of ideal objects indwelling in real objects of the films. For those who want to ground their theories of artistic representation in nominalism, it is always highly problematic just how such a sophisticated critical language could possibly have evolved given the textures of uniqueness they posit, and all of the conceptual problems that Husserl, Armstrong, and others have pointed out. With realism providing ontological grounding for a theory of representation, we shall see that many of the important questions of cinema may be addressed successfully.

The epistemology of cinematic representation

Contemporary film theory and criticism is permeated with an idealist epistemology. The criticism written about the film work of Nagisa Oshima will provide illustrative evidence of the critical practice that grows out of an idealist film theory. (In a moment we shall look at examples of that criticism.) With this body of idealist criticism in mind, it will be possible to indicate the epistemological disadvantages of idealism and the advantages for a realist account of cinematic representation.

When one reads criticism of the Oshima canon, a rather clearly defined conceptual map of the film experience emerges. A film is not an object of critics' perception. It is rather a locus for the depositing of images and sounds in the experience of spectators who, by means of imaginatively and ideologically grounded activity, *construct* the Oshima text. It is the text that has meaning and value; it is the locus for the representations. Text emerges out of an intersection of processes involving filmmaker and spectator activity reflecting broad cultural/social factors. This spectator–text relationship involves not only constitution of text by spectator but has the potential for authentic self-awareness, especially if the filmmaker contribution is that of an Oshima.

Thus, a spectator does not stand outside of an object called a film, perceiving its representations and other features, but rather may be, as described in the contemporary parlance, *inscribed within the text*, as active participant in realization of text. Moreover, in their activity, spectators utilize codes in order to construct the meaning and representations of the text; these codes include cinematic codes, cultural codes, individual filmmaker's codes, and so forth. Here are some examples of the Oshima criticism and how it fits the idealist mode.

Maureen Turim and John Mowitt,[1] in discussing the extraordinary opening sequence from *He Died after the War (Tokyo senso sengo hiwa* [a/k/a *The Story of the Man Who Left His Will on Film*]), utilize one of the assumptions – the nature of the film as an object of experience. The film is purportedly about two members of a Marxist film making cooperative, Motoki and Yasuko. In the opening sequence, Motoki – and we as spectators – seemingly see the suicide of another member of the cooperative named Endo (who leaps off a building) followed by the police being shown recovering Endo's camera and film footage. Next, however, we, and Motiki, see Endo alive. Turim and Mowitt regard the opening sequence as a kind of "false start," an experience that seems to get started then stops and starts again. They point to the seemingly unrelated nature of the visual and sound images that are presented together with the image burning out to a white absence.

It is the Turim–Mowitt analysis that this false start is part of a systematic effort by Oshima to structure the film so that it constitutes a "resistance to totalization which prevents us from conceiving of a film as a discrete critical object." In their view, the resistance to totalization functions "to collapse those categories of formal distinctions necessary to locate the critical object within a tradition of formalist classification."[2]

Turim and Mowitt go on to analyze the dual working of image frame and narrative strategy, arguing that they conspire to produce a certain kind of spectator positioning: "We are granted a subjective imaginary placement, a point of view on the scene, the beginnings of our imaginary position within the narrative."[3]

Paul Coates also finds resistance to totalization in the Oshima text, which threatens its status as having objecthood. He contends that it is more fruitful to model the Oshima film on the pattern of a nonsense sentence. The presence of contradiction in the Oshima text is the crucial determinate leading to this status for the film. As Coates puts it:

It is possible to see an Oshima film as a series of individual scenes that make sense when considered separately whilst overlooking the degree to which the whole they constitute is a nonsense sentence, a labyrinthine concatenation of incompatibilities. The viewer cannot totalize the film: there is no whole, only a series of parts, and so the whole film ... becomes a mystification ... it is experienced as such by the individual viewer, who is unable to master the contradictions the film embodies.[4]

Dana Polan, in dealing with the Oshima canon, explains how certain of the films are to be conceptualized:

Oshima's cinema suggests a way beyond the closures of representation: in these [films'] moments, the cinema ceases to be an art of viewers merely watching a complete[d] story to become instead a process in which spectators are called into play as historically rooted subjects who bring their own critical reactions to bear on the world of the film. Viewing becomes an active process in which spectator and cinema meet enabling the spectator to be changed by the encounter.[5]

The films that Polan has in mind are *In the Realm of the Senses (Ai no corrida)*, *Night and Fog in Japan (Nihon no yoru to kiri)*, and *Death by Hanging (Koshikei)*. As he sees it, in these films various strategies are utilized to enact "politics as a process between screen and spectator" and make "the process of figuration implicate the spectator."[6] In *Night and Fog in Japan*, Polan interprets the much criticized "theatrical effects" in the film as Brechtian alienation effects: They are events put in quotation marks; they constitute refusals to follow the conventions of dominant cinema; as such they are sites where "knowledge is passed between characters, aesthetic form, and the spectator."[7]

Polan is, thus, highlighting a number of relationships explicable in terms of the theory of spectator–text interaction. First, taking cinema as having a capacity to represent objects has involved closure, wherein the text is conceived of as a whole, a complete entity, with its meanings *in* it, and the relationship of viewer to it is that of a discoverer rather than a constructor of meaning. In such a view, the spectator is positioned passively, "merely watching a complete story" as Polan describes it. Peter Wollen has perhaps best described this feature:

Classical aesthetics always posited an essential unity and coherence to every work, which permitted a uniform and exhaustive decoding. Modernism disrupts this unity; it opens the work up, both internally and externally, outwards. Thus, there are no longer separate works, monads, each enclosed in its own individuality, a perfect globe, a whole.[8]

If we turn away from the classical aesthetic concept of the object as counseled, we conceive of the spectator as an active, historically rooted subject. Entailed is the notion that the spectator engages in the process of constituting the modernist text (e.g., an Oshima film). It follows that the spectator for a film like *Realm of the Senses* is not just anyone at any time at any place, but rather one whose historicity is actively mobilized in construction of the text. Correlatively, the Oshima text is not a representation of objects, events, and characters but rather a site where images are gathered so as to elicit spectator-shaping activity.

Ed Branigan, in analyzing *He Died after the War*, remarks on the constitutive activity of the spectator as follows: "Narration is a product of both a narrator and a reader; just as the text must create (inscribe) its reader, so a reader must create the text in its telling."[9] In the background of these proffered ways of conceiving the Oshima film is a theoretical shift vis-à-vis the nature of the work of art – a move away from conceiving of a film as an object and a move toward conceiving of a film as a site. Christian Metz describes this characteristic in the following observation:

The textual system, the interpretation of each film in its uniqueness, constitutes by definition a kind of mixed...site in which specific codes and nonspecific codes meet and combine one with another.[10]

To examine a work for its unity is thought unfortunate. Therefore, if it is a modernist or avant-garde text such as an Oshima film, it involves overlooking parts that do not fit or, as Wollen puts it, "ignoring gaps and fissures which exist in reality but are represented by an ideology characteristic of bourgeois society, which insists on the 'wholeness' and integrity of each individual consciousness."[11]

Thus, on the idealist view, the critic is urged to locate and give value to excesses, gaps, disruptions, and discontinuities. Where the bourgeois realist text strives to control and thoroughly discipline its own reading so that it can appear invariably as a solid unalterable object,[12] the avant-garde text of an Oshima film is a text that is really an intersection of processes that may produce, as Roland Barthes proposed, different structures of meaning on every occasion of its being "read."[13]

Further, both Turim and Mowitt and Stephen Heath take it as central to an analysis of the Oshima text that an identification be made of spectator positioning within the text. In discussing the reflexivity that abounds in *He Died after the War*, Turim and Mowitt argue that:

We are not simply confronted by mise-en-abîme, a series of frames within frames, reflected in a single mirror which easily reconstitutes the subject's spectators as "I." We find that we are perhaps not at the center. Where are we in this film?[14]

Stephan Heath, in interpreting *In the Realm of the Senses*, speaks of the centrality of the following questions—"Where are you in this film? and what is this film like for you to be there?"[15] One feature Heath identifies in that part of the film that involves looking at looking is that the spectator is seen in the seeing of the sexual. Heath analyzes what he calls the apparatus of look and identification as "a specific construction (not a natural reproduction, a simple reflection)...[that involves] a splitting of the seen turns on the development of a divided inclusion of the spectator."[16] Branigan, in pinpointing the spectator–text relationship in *He Died after the War*, argues that "just as it [the film] constructs inconsistent characters, the text constructs an inconsistent spectator." Correlatively, the director "must construct (inscribe) a certain kind of spectator for the text. . . . [T]he spectator must be constituted as an unseen observer viewing the space from possible locations *in* the fictional scene."[17] Branigan points up what he takes to be "many shots from camera positions which are impossible for the perfect spectator to occupy." He gives an illustration from *He Died after the War:*

We see a shot from the position of a wall, a high angle crane shot in the middle of a wide highway, and a shot of a character looking out from the top of a tall building, but from a position on the other side of the railing – suspended over empty space. Oshima uses such shots systematically.[18]

Branigan also contends that "impossible spectator positions are . . . related to impossible POV shots." He gives as an example:

When Motoki chases the police car through the streets and into a tunnel, we soon realize that the shots from his view are moving much too fast and it should be impossible for him to keep up with the car.[19]

Discovery versus construction

It is characteristic of the foregoing analyses of the Oshima oeuvre that the critical commentary is usually correct and insightful, but the underlying theory utilized to assess the significance of the critical work lends distortion to our grasp of the features identified. We will start with the presence of contradiction in the Oshima film and its connection with the alleged status of the aesthetic object following from it.

Contradiction. Underlying Paul Coates's interpretation is an especially prevalent confusion about the notion of contradiction in contemporary film theory. The term *contradiction* has two central senses. One posits contradiction as a *property of a statement*; the other makes contradiction a *property of an action*. It is important to keep these two senses separate; in Coates's commentary on Oshima, these two senses become conflated with the consequence that an understanding of the Oshima film is obscured.

As a property of a statement, contradiction is indeed centrally related to nonsense. In no case may it be asserted, for example, that "Kichi is and is not a man at the same time, in the same place, and in the same respect." No one including Marx, who is primarily responsible for the other sense of "contradiction," would ever propose that a contradictory statement is anything but nonsense or that a state of affairs could exist that is describable via a contradictory statement.[20]

As a property of an action, contradiction may be a characteristic of an existing state of affairs, for example, "contradictions are inherent in capitalism" and a statement involving such contradiction may be meaningful.[21] Coates conflates these two meanings of "contradiction" when he invites us to regard the Oshima film on the model of "a non-sense sentence, a labyrinthine concatenation of incompatibles. The viewer cannot totalize the film: there is no whole, only a series of parts."[22]

The manner in which repetition of incompatibilities is structured in the Oshima film canon leads the spectator to have to cope with contradiction as an action property. The spectator must become active in imaginatively forming, as it were, a conceptual map of the whole in a way not required in the experience of the typical Hollywood thriller. The spectator is not, however, restricted to an experience of a series of parts; spectators may form conceptions of the whole even so. *Realm of the Senses,* however riddled with contradiction as an action property, is nevertheless the object of spectators' experience; there is a totalizing aspect to the experience. That is, the film as an object of experience has the capacity to position the spectator to be unable to master its contradictions as properties of actions. Having capacities to so position spectators is just as much a property of a film as its visual or sound features.

Codes. There are reasons why the notion of perception under codes at a site called a film is not a fruitful notion. First, the concept of the film as being not an object with certain meanings, representations, and aesthetic features but rather a site where construction using codes takes place involves an unnecessary conceptual move. Apparently, this conceptual shift is deemed necessary in order to account for the ideologically affective character of works (among other reasons). The dominant ideology is thought to be working through films to position capitalist subjects. Films are made by the dominant cinema, with seamless editing and other such strategies, in order to reproduce capitalist subjects. If the film is conceived of as an object with its meanings *in* the object, then this vital affective dimension is thought to be lost. To examine a film for its unity is regarded as unfortunate, for instance, because it involves overlooking parts that do not fit, as we have seen Wollen put it:

[Overlooking] gaps and fissures which exist in reality but are repressed by an ideology characteristic of bourgeois society which insists on the "wholeness" and "integrity" of each individual consciousness.[23]

Wollen, in discussing the process of decoding in film, says:

No longer an empty treasure house waiting to receive its treasure, the mind becomes productive. . . . The old image of the reader as consumer is broken.[24]

It is, however, important to realize that the same observations about the working of ideology in film and through film experience may be made without abandoning the concept of a film as an object with properties that may be discovered by prepared observers.

A distinction between occurrent and dispositional properties is one we would ordinarily make with respect to any object in the world. Its extension to the case of film experience makes possible the preservation of the notion that a film is an object. Occurrent properties are those that one senses in the moment, they *occur* in the moment. Dispositional properties, by contrast, are ones that last over time. For example, a sugar cube is white, makes a certain sound when tapped on a hard surface, tastes sweet, and so forth. These features are occurrent properties of sugar. Sugar, like any other object, has certain dispositional properties, for example, it will dissolve in water.

Films also have occurrent and dispositional properties. Their visual and sound features are their occurrent properties. Visual properties would include camera position, camera movement, and editing. Sound properties would include sound texture, sound quality, sound mix, and so forth. In addition to these properties, films also have powers or dispositions to affect different audiences differently. Godard's dislocation affects are best understood as dispositional properties. For example, given the kind of experiences audiences had had prior to his 1959 film, *Breathless* (*A bout de souffle*) would have the power to dislocate the audience from the time and space of the film.

Early in the film, Michel (played by Jean-Paul Belmondo) is chased by the police. In portraying the chase, Godard crosses the 180° line while quickening the pace drastically. For 1959 audiences, used to having a vivid sense of the geography in which an action occurs and an easy grasp of the various stages of an act, the police chase sequence dislocated them from the filmic space and time.

Films have dispositions to affect our senses of things, for example, the nature of the space and time in *Breathless* is that of dislocation; films have dispositions to affect our feelings; identification is aroused in the audience during the early sequences of *Breathless* only to be undercut later; dispositional properties are just as much properties of the object, whether it be a cube of sugar or a film, as are the occurrent properties. That the way in which films ideologically position their spectators (e.g., position them to be reproduced as capitalist subjects) involves going "outside" the object, the film, to consider a relational property, in no way justifies attributing the capacity to position an audience to something other than the film. Just as the capacity to dissolve in water is a dispositional property of sugar, so the capacity to position spectators productively or unproductively is a property of the object, the film.

Given this distinction between occurrent and dispositional properties and its applicability to conceptualize film, we can see that there is no reason to denigrate unity nor reason to fault the process of interpreting films because we must take into account relational properties of the film, for example, its capacities to position spectators in certain ideologically grounded ways. It may be that films with disunified characters are of great interest in the way they reflect the "gaps and fissures" in human existence. It is quite another thing, however, to brand the realist epistemology false to the ideological implications of cinema because it posits an object of perception when in fact there is only a site where construction takes place using codes.

Second, the utilization of the concept of a code to identify the mode of construction in which the perceiver engages while experiencing a film is not a fruitful approach. The material with which both critic and spectator deal in recognizing representations is of such a nature that using codes, in the sense utilized in contemporary film theory, is precluded. There are at least two uses of "code" in film criticism. One of them is unproblematic: "The guys in the black hats in the Western are the bad guys." Here "code" is used as a stand-in for "convention." We know that the generalization "the guys with the black hats in the Western are the bad guys," is false; but, as a rule of thumb – as a convention – one often follows in making and understanding a Western, it serves our purposes. The other meaning of "code" demands rigor. The notion of a systematic code was introduced in order to counter the impressionistic criticism that had marked earlier forms of criticism; instead of using vague references to how such and such a form or content seems to a critic, the systematic code is supposed to get at what is in fact at work in the filmmakers' activity.

Systematic codes are generalizations that are true for all those cases to which they are applied. Thus, Godard's use of jump cutting to dislocate the spectator from the time of the film would be thought to be part of his code. When we perceive the Godard film, we perceive it under the code of dislocation. In this way, we sense the systematic way in which the film is structured.

A generalization would be expressed in an if–then proposition: If such and such conditions are satisfied, then the object has so and so feature. For example, if a cube of sugar is immersed in water at a specified temperature range, in a controlled environment of a certain type, then the sugar will dissolve.

However, the identifications that an audience makes about a film – its value, its ideological meaning, its capacities to position spectators, its representations – admit of a total relevance factor. Thus, to recognize the capacities of *Breathless* to position spectators productively requires that the perceiver take into account all of the possible ways in which features of the film may be utilized. Every visual, every sound, every affect of the film can, depending on the context, make a difference as to what the ideological meaning of the film will be and what objects are represented by the film. In the case of a film, no feature may be separated out as *not* being relevant for a determination of what is represented. In no other discourse do we face this total relevance factor. In other judgments we make, we can always separate out most features as irrelevant for the judgment, a fact that makes it possible to formulate and use systematically assembleable generalizations in these nonart cases. But film shares with all the arts this special situation that a total relevance factor prevents the use of generalizations.

For instance, only a very few features are relevant for determining whether or not a glass will hold water, for example, its possession of a solid bottom and side, a surface that will resist various environmental pressures of certain standard sorts, and so forth. The kind of design on its surface would be irrelevant, just how big or small it is, its shape, its color, and so forth, all would be separable out as irrelevant for making the judgment whether or not it could hold water. If cinesemiology is to provide precision in place of the vagueness of impressionistic criticism, its codes must be generalizations. These generalizations must tell the readers of criticism what characteristics films have: If such and such conditions are satisfied, then the film positions the spectators in such and such a way or has so and so representations. A necessary condition for using generalizations such as codes is that the total relevance factor *not* be operative in the discourse. This is so because when the total relevance factor is operative, generalizations become far too complicated to be utilized.

For instance, suppose you are told that there is a murder sequence in *Breathless* that was dislocational for its 1959 audience. You do not see the sequence where Michel kills a policeman, but the critic tells you of the instancing of the codes, the relevant generalizations governing Godard's act of cinematic expression. The example is apt because if systematic coding is to be more than just a rule of thumb – false but useful in some cases – we should be able to know that the sequence is dislocational without relying on intuition, for example, directly seeing the feature (as will be discussed in the section on intuition and transcendence). A phenomenology of the film experience will reveal the implausibility of there being code-governed features of films. A moment's reflection on the overwhelming complexity of such a generalization will substantiate the claim that systematic coding is inappropriate for critical communication between critics and their readers. If the character Michel steals a car in the opening sequences of the film and is then chased by police in the next sequence, the sequence will be dislocational only if camera work, mise-en-scène, editing, and so forth, are used in a specific way in the opening sequence and the audience had specific expectations, beliefs, sensibilities, prior experiences with art and film, and so forth.

In order for successful critical communication, just think how incredibly complex the descriptions would have to be about camera placement, camera angle, camera movement, actor's look, actresses's gesture, sound texture, sound quality, sound mix, music editing, editing, pace, and so forth. A phenomenology of the experience of the opening sequences of *Breathless* would reveal that each directorial choice created in portraying Michel from the very beginning of the film plus how the police look, how the environment looks, and so forth, would be relevant for making a judgment about whether a sequence is dislocational.

To tell someone just which camera positions were used in the opening sequence and in the subsequent chase sequence (including Michel's ride down the country road) would require giving names to each possible camera position. To say that the 180° line is crossed at a certain point in the chase, as important as it is for dislocation, is not sufficient to ensure dislocation, since the line is crossed in many circumstances in many films, yet dislocation does not occur. Editing, pace, music, camera angle, mise-en-scène, and countless other features all conspire to create the dislocating affect. To give names to each of the camera positions, to each of the editing practices, and so forth would prove worthless to the act of critical communication. No one could ever remember such a generalization much less use it. Without names for each of the features involved in building the dislocation affect, there is no generalization, no code, involved. The complication is just too immense. For example, suppose we try to use the following generalization: "If camera position of such and such a sort is used, and lighting of so and so a type is used, if pace is quickened just so much, etc., then the chase sequence will dislocate an audience with such and such characteristics of expectation, belief, sensibility, and with such and such prior experience with art and movies," where in each case we described just the camera position, lighting, pace, and so forth used in *Breathless* and where we described the expectations and other factors of reception for the 1959 audience. Such a generalization would fulfill the requirements that systematic coding must satisfy but no one would use it.[25]

Critical communication, the act of critics writing to their readers, involves the use of all of the communicative skills at the critics' disposal to guide the readers to perceive what the critics have perceived in the film. By use of vivid images, metaphors, similes, whatever, the critics enable their readers to intuit in the film for themselves what the critics have at a prior time intuited, for example, recognize the capacity of the film to dislocate its audience. As Arnold Isenberg pointed out: "Reading criticism otherwise than in the presence of the work of art, whether directly or in vivid recollection, is a blank and senseless employment."[26]

In the case of film (and the arts in general), a phenomenology of film experience reveals that what we have is a situation in which we have *more qualities than we have names for;* that is, the qualities that contribute to certain types of affect or representation are far too numerous to make it worth our while to give them names. Without names for affect-making features or for representation-making features, we can never formulate and utilize generalizations, that is, only with named features can we hold that when so and so features are present, then the subject will be affected in such and such a way or the object have such and such representations. The features that make sequence have representations or affects are neither unique nor general enough (in most cases) to permit their naming. They are in-between qualities. Critics can activate their readers' intuitive processes so that they grasp these in-between qualities. Only by being led to look and hear and feel and have senses of things can critical communication succeed in communicating about affect and representation (of a complex and significant sort).

Representations in film would have a varying status with respect to the total relevance factor and hence to whether generalizations could be used to identify them. Some aspects of depictions would be so easy to identify that only a limited few characteristics would have to be known, for example, whether such and such a character in *Breathless* is a man or a woman. Critics could communicate to their readers that the motion picture depicts a man as its protagonist, relying on standard notions of maleness to make the identification. For any of the more significant and complex representations, for example, how Michel in *Breathless* is portrayed, attempts at using coding would encounter the total relevance factor, which would render useless the semiotic system for making sense of the representation. The more complicated cases of representations are the ones that a cinesemiotics is intended to illuminate, but the system would not be able to do so. Fortunately, we have the ability to utilize intuition; fortunately, critics have the writing skills to activate our intuitive processes so that we can grasp complex portrayal and symbolic relationships in the motion pictures we experience and that they write about. Intuitively we grasp recurring features, for example, dislocation-making features in *Breathless*. Although they are recurring but not unique, recurring but not general enough to permit naming and hence generalizing about, they are discoverable by prepared spectators using their intuitive capacities.

Whereas contemporary film theory (with its idealist/nominalist leanings) has wanted to make our apprehension of representations a process wherein we decode signs (images and sounds) in a way governed by codes, phenomenology (with its realist epistemology) makes the apprehension of representations in motion pictures a process of recognizing via intuition features of objects, events, persons, and states of affairs, whether these objects be real or fictional.

Detextualizing film criticism

The term *text* has been introduced into the film critics' language in order to mark the commonality of circumstances in which the appreciator of both literature and film is situated. Previously, it was thought that in the case of literature the appreciators deal first with signs (i.e., words), then second are led to imagine objects (i.e., they read), while in the case of cinema appreciators directly apprehend objects (i.e., they are perceivers). Now, with the constructivist model governing conceptualization of the cinematic exeperience, it is thought that in both appreciation of literature and appreciation of film, the situation is much the same; appreciators are confronted in both cases by signs (in cinema they are images and sounds) that must be decoded in a process of reading. Text is that which becomes constituted via the interaction of sign recognition and decoding activity as well as construction of meaning by spectators.

Utilizing this textual model for the film experience, the Oshima film seems to include the spectator in an especially active way in constituting text. Hence, it is thought felicitous to characterize the experiential situation as one where spectator is constructor of the text. By contrast, the so-called bourgeois realist text presents an invariable object, that is, one where signifier and signified are transparently related, one where spectator is positioned into passivity.

In considering the Oshima oeuvre, we find the same gaps and fissures and excesses to which Wollen gives emphasis. Confronting them does indeed foster activity on the part of spectators. In Oshima's *Boy* (*Shonen*), gaps are very much a part of the experience. The film is about a family who preys upon unsuspecting auto drivers. Members of the family fake accidents with the drivers' cars, then threaten legal action unless hush money is paid. The structure of fakery permeates the film to such an extent that it is perceived as "overused." Such overuse arouses our recognition of the presence of the cinematic apparatus. The father has fake wounds, the family's profession is fakery, the boy is taught how to fake wounds (his father even injects him with a chemical substance to give the fake appearance of bruises). The manner of shooting in one scene implicates Japan in this process of fakery; the red and white colors of the Japanese flag are connected with the family project of fakery.

In one sequence, the protagonist, the boy of the title, goes away. We feel that he may no longer be able to relate to what his family is doing to him and to these drivers. He is able to obtain a ticket to a distant location. We see him arrive in a town, walk through the town, finally sitting down by a shore. We sit with him for a long time by the shore. Our feeling is that he is a runaway. Suddenly, the boy is back with his parents, standing in front of a map in still another town square, planning still another assault on unsuspecting drivers. Left out are the boy's return trip, his parents' reaction to his return, and an explanation of why he returned. In short, a gap is opened up in the narrative line that upsets our emotional relationship to the boy and his circumstances.

Oshima has structured the sequence very carefully to provide us with an abundance of detail. As the boy prepares to leave, we see him button each and every button on his clothes; when he sits by the shore, film time becomes assimilated to real time. This structuring cultivates a sense of seeing everything; suddenly this sense is shattered; a gap in our experience needs filling but, Oshima will not fill it for us. In *Boy*, it is also evident that excessive portrayal has been deliberately included. In one scene, the protagonist knocks over a snowman. We are shown his action not only in slow motion but he performs the action over and over again.

Eventually, the family reaches Hokkaido, the uppermost island in the Japanese chain. The boy says: "This is the end of Japan; only outer space is left," implying that their activity across the face of the entire country is connected with the nature of the country. As you experience this overly obvious symbolism, sensitive to his sheer deliberateness, you have to wonder how to take it; by realizing its connection with reflexivity and exposing the operations of the cinematic apparatus, its purpose comes into view.

The manner in which Oshima's *Boy* concludes counters established norms governing our experience of the cinema. The ending of *Boy* engages the spectators' sensibilities and expectations developed from experience with the dominant cinema. As spectators try to relate to this ending, which is, in a sense, not an ending, they come into contact with the expectations that naturally arise in connection with a film's ending. The family is finally captured by the police. We see them struggle to resist capture. Then we see them in freeze-frame seated on a train with off-screen narration telling of their personal histories from birth to the present. We feel that the film is now ending. Their adventure is over. Conventions for ending a film with a factual basis like *Boy* (the film was derived from an actual incident reported in the newspaper) are being observed, given the way the still-shot of the family in the train and off-screen narration proceed. We feel that it is a slice of life rendition. But then when we are brought up to date on this slice of life, the film continues. The train continues to move, the boy talks to someone next to him. The experience of *Boy* continues; a close-up of the boy, for the first time in the film, arouses our sympathy in a way that such a positioning had avoided earlier. We do not experience a rounded whole as the substance of our experience. Oshima has set up our expectations for a unified experience and then subverted those expectations.

The gaps, excesses, and incompleteness in Oshima's *Boy* require an active spectator, but there is no need to posit a constructing spectator who forms a text in order to account for the presence of these features. Instead, they are dispositional properties of Oshima's *Boy* to position spectators to have a sense of gaps in the narrative, to find the style of expression excessive, to have difficulty in laying out a coherent conceptual map of the film's action, and to feel the experience unfulfilling. Such dispositional properties aim to position spectators who typically relate to films in terms of the kind of norms of comprehension and reaction elucidated by David Bordwell,[27] that is, classical American narrative norms, art cinema narrative norms, and so forth. (In Chapter II, the role of norms that Bordwell delineates will be examined from a phenomenological standpoint.) These relational properties of *Boy* are just as much properties of any Oshima film as its occurrent properties, that is, its visual/sound complexes. In discovering the affective relationships fostered by the film, spectators need to be quite active but need not construct any meanings.

Moreover, the manner in which the occurrent/dispositional properties of the film came to be present in the work is not the burning issue it has often been thought to be. It seems obvious that critics will sometimes be able to discover connections in a film that the filmmakers did not think of when engaged in the creative process of making the film. Hence, it is not necessary to decide whether *authorial intention* should be the locus of evidence for a film's meaning or whether the critics' activity in constructing text ought to be the source for critical judgment. In whatever manner the properties of a film found their way into the work, they are there, to be discovered by spectators who are prepared and imaginative enough to successfully engage in the highly active process of discovering the properties of a film via intuition in the sense Husserl specifies. (Husserl's concept of intuition will be explained in the next section.) That the properties of a film are to be discovered rather than constructed does not entail that there is only one interpretation of a film or that judgments about their presence are free from error. There is still room for a film to admit of many interpretations as well as for equally prepared and imaginative critics to disagree about the nature of its properties. That judgments about the meaning and representations of a film will always be subject to error on the realist model should be viewed as an advantage. Would we not want a fruitful modeling of the critics' activity to entail that critical interpretation is a fallible process? As has been apparent, the phenomenological model developed here is objectivist in nature. Though spectators may sometimes error in their discovery process, the *status* of their activity as discoverers of objectively existing properties of films is not thereby called into question.

Spectator positioning

With the move away from conceptualizing any Oshima film as a set of visuals and sounds that provoke spectator construction of an entity called the text and movement toward it being conceptualized as an object of experience, the nature of spectator positioning in the act of knowing has a quite different character. Whereas the commentaries have spectators inscribed in the text, constructed as inconsistent spectators, placed in impossible points of view, realism has spectator positioning being a function of dispositional properties of the object – the film – which precludes these unnecessary ways of describing the nature of reception.

Take, for instance, Branigan's example of the impossible point of view in *He Died after the War*. Motoki may not be able to keep up with the speeding police car as he chases it through Tokyo streets; also we may not be able to see events suspended over empty space. In a fictional context, however, these viewpoints may be presented without any reason to label them impossible. It is merely a contingent fact that we cannot run as fast as a police car or hang suspended over empty space; impossibility is quite another matter. In a similar vein, the notion that Oshima grants the spectator the status of "unseen observer viewing the space from possible locations in the fictional scene," is not really the point. We may feel like we are in the space; we may identify with a point of view hanging above the action of the film from the space comprising the fictional scene. The concept of the spectator being inscribed in the text is unacceptable because the spectator's relationship to the film's action is always one of being an observer, discoverer, and responder with an accompanying marginal awareness of separation between self and object even when psychical distance is broken down and psychical immersion is the mode of response.

As has become apparent, the conceptual moves seemingly warranted by the emergence of the Oshima canon (and ones like it) are really unnecessary. Oshima's cinema is *not* a further indication of the constructedness of all filmic articulation. It *is*, however, a cinema that positions spectators to reflect upon crucial features of their experience of cinema's place in societies with specific histories and underlying ideologies of certain sorts. Isn't that enough?

Transaction, transparency, and transcendence

As we have seen, contemporary film theory proposes that depiction, portrayal, and symbolism arise out of a *transaction* of spectator with text: as such, cinematic representations are constructions by the spectator in response to the images and sounds they experience at a film screening. By contrast to this transactional view of cinematic representation, phenomenology posits the spectator as a discoverer not a constructor of cinematic representations: depictions, portrayals, and instances of symbolism that he or she apprehends in the motion picture exist independently of his or her acts of grasping them. Accordingly, phenomenology's theory is one of transcendence, that is, representations transcend the conscious acts involved in their apprehension.

Husserlian modeling of representation may be seen to occupy a middle-ground position between the transactionalism so often found in contemporary film theory and a transparency theory most prominently championed by André Bazin. In Bazin's view spectators in apprehending cinematic representation confront objects that stand in a transparent relationship with reality; when we apprehend what a motion picture depicts, we see through the film object to the real object.

Transparency has been a crucial concept for many influential theories of photographic representation. The basic notion underlying the view is that the film image bears a transparent relationship to reality. Often the image of a window is elicited to explain the transparency involved. As spectators, in relating to the real via photography, we are positioned before a window through which we look at the things themselves.

According to Bazin, film image is to be "evaluated not according to what it adds to reality but what it reveals of it."[1] "The photographic image is the object itself, the object freed from the conditions of time and space that govern it."[2] "The photograph as such and the object in itself share a common being, after the fashion of a fingerprint."[3] Additionally, Bazin places much emphasis upon photography's capacity to reproduce reality automatically: "For the first time an image of the world is formed automatically, without the creative intervention of man.... All the arts are based on the presence of man, only photography derives an advantage from his absence."[4] "Accordingly, the aesthetic qualities of photography are to be sought in its power to lay bare the realities."[5]

Thus, at one end of a continuum of representation theory, a hyperrealist such as Bazin wants to assimilate depiction, portrayal, and symbolism to the pattern of everyday life perception of an independently existing object with the motion picture a transparent entity through which we see the things themselves. At the other end of the continuum, we find the transactional view of contemporary film theory wherein representation is a by-product of an interaction between subject and object in which representations are constructions out of the contents of mental acts divorced from an externally existing object.

By contrast with transparency and transactional theories, phenomenology provides instead a realist theory preserving (1) the transactional sense of mediation in the process of recognizing representation and (2) the transparency sense of the independence of the object represented.

The transparency problematic

For the transparency theorist such as Bazin, because of the automatic reproducibility of photography, the motion picture allows spectators to look through a transparent medium at reality. Such a view seems insupportable. Photography is but one element in the complex filmmaking process and may involve distortion of reality. Editing also plays a crucial role in cinematic representation. To maintain that an alleged capacity of photography to capture the things photographed via its automatic operation presumes that editing is simply a process of joining together shots that show the things themselves. It is clear, however, that editing plays a formative role in the representation of objects, not simply the function of connecting shots together.

Orson Welles was an exemplar for Bazin's transparency theory. Take the opening sequence from Welles's *Touch of Evil*. If it is considered only as a long take, one may have the false impression that the sequence confirms the notion that the automatic reproducibility of cinematography can capture the real and deliver it up to our experience.

The opening sequence show the setting of a time bomb in the trunk of a car, a couple driving the car across the Mexican–American border, and the life at the border at that time. Using the long-take style seems to preserve Bazinian realist values;[6] the integrity of the space and time in which the event occurs is maintained (editing would have supposedly disrupted the flow of the event and presented only spatial fragments, not the whole space); scope is given for the spectator to discover the meanings present in the space and time (rather than have his or her perception directed to meanings).

If, however, one looks more deeply into the experience of the opening sequences in *Touch of Evil*, it becomes apparent that transparency and automatic reproducibility are neither so unproblematically nor so clearly involved in the values of the film experience. As we first see Vargas and his wife Suzie (Charlton Heston and Janet Leigh, respectively) walking along the street toward the border where the car with its time bomb is headed, there could as easily have been a cut as a continuation of the long take as far as cinematic representation is concerned. The shot is a great tour de force but, for purposes of what the sequence represents, there would be no loss of knowledge of what is depicted, portrayed, or symbolized if there had been a cut at this point. Bazin is developing a theory of cinematic representation partly by reference to the film making stylistics of directors such as Welles and Wyler, de Sica, and Renoir. The same may be said for other parts of the bombing event portrayed with the long take, for example, Heston and Leigh stand next to the car with the bomb talking with the border guard.

When the long take ends with the kiss between Heston and Leigh, followed immediately by a cut to the car exploding (seemingly timed with the kiss), editing assumes a primary role in portrayal of subsequent events. Heston and Leigh's reactions to the car exploding is an event just as placing the bomb and the bomb going off were events yet it is shown primarily via editing, not via a long take. The efforts of the local community to cope with the explosion aftermath are intercut with Heston and Leigh deciding what to do, then separating with plans to meet later. As local authorities talk about what happened, identifying the victims of the bombing takes place, and notice of the arrival of Hank Quinlan, the local police authority (played by Welles himself), is registered, extensive editing into these actions characterizes the style of presentation.

Thus, if Welles's *Touch of Evil* were offered as paradigmatic of effective cinematic representation, not only the opening long take but the subsequent sequence (the bombing aftermath) must be taken into account in the analysis; this broader perspective would not sustain a claim that the long-take style is *responsible* for the effectiveness of the portrayal.

Deep focus is another vector in the Bazinian realist framework. With this feature of photography, the audience gains a vivid sense of the space in which an action occurs as well as an opportunity to look about the space to discover for oneself what relationships exist (rather than be overly guided in one's looking). Setting the time bomb at the opening of the long take is highlighted to the minimizing of the background, which seems most appropriate for portraying the event represented at that moment in the sequence. In the explosion aftermath, deep focus is used only where the action calls for it: There are some shots where emphasis on foreground discussions among authorities in the community at the border takes precedence over background objects. By putting objects or persons in the foreground, filmmakers may indicate relationships of, for example, dominance as when Hank Quinlan first appears in the film, shown in an upward angle with his image filling the frame grotesquely.

Bazin's analogy between filmic representation and fingerprints or molds or decals is not convincing. A decal merely reproduces the shape, the outward form, or any design that may be on the surface of objects. Bazin, however, speaks about spectator capacity to ferret out the inner life of character as a value of long-take style – discovering intentions, desires, feelings. A fingerprint similarly only deals with the outward characteristics of objects.

A counterinstance to Bazinian theory may be found in Visconti's adaptation of *Death in Venice* (*Morte a Venezia*). In this film, long lenses are used to distort the outward appearances of characters and settings in order to call attention to features of the inner life of the characters. Early in the film, when Aschenbach first encounters the young boy, Tadzio, about whom he becomes increasingly attached, long lenses make it look as though they are physically apart when in fact they have been in close proximity. Later in the film, long lenses give the opposite effect, indicative of the change in their relationship. Tadzio now seems very close as Aschenbach follows him obsessively through Venice streets. A shift in camera position reveals that they have been quite far apart. Psychic closeness between Aschenbach and Tadzio has replaced psychic distance. The distortion of outward appearance has been the vehicle for revelation of inner realities. The analogy of cinematic representation with decals, fingerprints, or molds could not accommodate such cases.

Automatic reproduction does not have the role in representation that Bazin believes it to have. Suppose one grants that the hand of the artist does not intervene between object and image as it does in the case of the painter, sculptor, or writer. In cinematography, if we simply turn on the camera and simply point it at some object, it is true that a representation of the object is produced. In writing or painting or sculpting, the artist cannot be so passive; such artists must be extremely active in order to produce any image that represents the object.

Such a distinction between cinematography and other creative artistic activities, however, constitutes a distinction without a difference. Cinematography, if utilized simply automatically, produces nothing of artistic quality in its representations. To merely point the camera at an object may have the purity Bazin mentions but no *significant* connection with representation follows. No cases of cinematic representation that any adequate theory would have to take into account in order to properly explain representation was ever accomplished in the "pure" way of simple automatic reproduction.

Let us suppose another type of case involving representation accomplished via motion picture photography and the other arts. An event is registered by all the arts: Vargas and Suzie in *Touch of Evil* walk to the Mexican–American border. A totally inexperienced cameraperson records the event; an accomplished painter renders a portrait; an expert novelist writes a sketch of the event. The automatic reproducibility of the motion picture is maximized. Do we have confidence that the motion picture will be the most faithful rendering of the event? Will it be asymptotic to reality?[7] Would we not think it likely that the non–motion picture renderings of the event will be more faithful?

There may be an existential connection between what we see and something that was before the camera during the shooting phase, but it is far from clear that anything of significance issues from this connection. What was before the camera may have been a performance by actors, with the event portrayed by the film only fully realized once the editing process is complete. Moreover, the highly complex process of cinematography cannot be characterized as "purely automatic": Decisions about how to capture what is before the camera are ubiquitous. If the real object represented is an aspect of the inner life – intention, desire, feeling, belief – using a means that automatically operates may be quite irrelevant to its portrayal.

For the late-1940s sensibility, after the artificiality of the Italian white telephone films and Hollywood escapist fare, after World War II and in the midst of its aftermath, the characters of *Shoeshine* may have seemed as Bazin put it "overwhelmingly real,"[8] but this audience's perception has nothing to do with realism an as epistemological doctrine. Bazin was not always able to keep realism as an epistemological doctrine and realism as a style in art separate. Realist theory asserts the independence of the objects represented by the motion picture from the knowing mind. Cinematic realism as a style in film history has taken many different forms; Lumière's capturing of the train coming into the station, Pabst's German street films, the poetic realism of Carné, and the neorealism of de Sica's *Shoeshine*.

Bazin makes much of the amalgam[9] utilized in Italian neorealism (the productive mixture of nonactors and actors) to capture a sense of the real. He speaks of the spontaneity that issues from shooting in the streets rather than creating events that exist on the studio floor, supposedly a real-making feature. With the distance provided by half a century, *Shoeshine*'s characters neither seem overwhelmingly real nor do the situations seem to have greater verisimilitude for being shot in the streets rather than on a set. But even if the characters and situations did cultivate a powerful sense of realism in the audience, the issues of epistemological realism would remain separate. Italian neorealism did not have an "aesthetic of reality" as Bazin terms it but rather an aesthetic of a realist style. Films with only professional actors may just as surely guide spectator perception to *the* objects represented by a motion picture representation.

Intuition and transcendence

Husserl's transcendence theory escapes the objections to which a Bazinian realist theory is susceptible.[10] A strength of the phenomenological model is its preservation of the intuitive richness of those acts in which we apprehend what an art object represents. When perceivers intuit properties of an object, they directly apprehend those properties: No inference is made from the sensa to properties of objects. Phenomenological theory makes apprehension of representation a direct process. A paradigm case of intuition is usually thought to be one in which, for example, a woman blind from birth cannot know what it is for an object to be yellow; no one can explain it to her. There is nothing that anyone could say from which she could *infer* that an object is yellow. She will have to acquire sight in order to know what a yellow object is.

Husserl's theory of intuition goes beyond this kind of case while maintaining directness at the core of intuition. He explains that acts of sense perception are direct acts, that is, acts that are not founded upon other acts, directed on other objects (*LI*, 787ff). The striking aspect of Husserl's theory for twentieth-century thinking about perception, with its passionate leanings toward idealism, is that

the object itself is actually put before us in such a manner that that object is *itself* the subject of psychical activity.[11]

In recognizing what the Dürer engraving depicts, the real knight is put before us; he is the object of our act. We directly apprehend him. It is also the case that in such apprehension a complex process involving the mediation by the noema, noesis, hyle, horizon, and so forth obtains. According to Husserl, when and insofar as the qualities of our sensa and of our object as intended are identical, we have an intuition of the object (PS, 304). It may have seemed, with all of the talk about the mediating role of the noema/noesis, that the object in itself, for example, the real knight, could not possibly "be put before us" or be "the object of our psychic activity," but such directness of apprehension is precisely what Husserl wants. As complex and difficult as intuition is, as highly mediated a process as it is, it nevertheless involves the object itself being what we grasp. For Husserl, there is no incompatibility between directness and mediation via the noema, noesis, hyletic data, and horizon because the former and latter *arise together*.

Husserl offers the following picture of intuition, which applies to apprehending artistic representations. Consciousness intends an object: the bombing in *Touch of Evil*. This cognitive act is a complex whole, with parts intentionally directed upon corresponding elements— parts, properties, or relations – in its object. Consciousness intends a bombing; parts include setting the bomb, the drive to the border with the bomb inside, Heston and Leigh walking beside the car, and so forth. If and insofar as those elements are only intended and not themselves present to the mind, the cognitive act is a *mere* representation. Husserl describes the cognitive act as a

web of partial intentions, fused together in the unity of a single total intention directed upon the object, as the *only* way in which we can...understand how consciousness reaches out beyond what is actually lived through: how it can, so to speak, mean beyond itself, and the meaning can be fulfilled. (*LI*, 701)

Husserl is saying that as we "pass through" the various moments forming the act – hyletic, noematic, and noetic – intending an object of the act is taking place, involving partial intentions. As we experience the opening long take in *Touch of Evil,* we are intending the bombing while also intending a relationship between the Heston and Leigh characters and the occupants of the car with the bomb, intending sinister forces in the environment, and so forth, all fused into an overall intention – a bomb set in one place is going to go off in another.

Fulfillment is obviously a crucial notion in Husserl's concept of intuition. The fulfillment relation must be experiences of the same thing. That which is thought to be such and such must be the very thing that it is found to be. Husserl urges the perspective that the operation of intuition and the movement toward fulfillment are highly complex and difficult processes even though, in the sense specified, there is a directness of apprehension involved:

If we imaginatively envisage an object turning it to every side, our sequence of images is constantly linked by syntheses of fulfillment in respect of its *partial* intentions, but each new image presentation does not, as a whole, fulfill its predecessor, nor does the whole series progressively approach any goal.... Gain and loss are balanced at every step: a new act has richer fullness in regard to certain properties for whose sake it has lost fullness in regard to others. (*LI*, 721)

In the opening long take in *Touch of Evil,* we intend the bombing from the first. We do not move toward an inference that there will be a bombing; we have seen the bomb set. As we see the event unfold, our intuitive experience is fulfilling what we intended. Fulfillment occurs only where there is a self-conscious realization that what was merely thought of becomes intuitively present *as* it was thought to be.

What the mere intention means, but presents only in a more or less inauthentic and inadequate manner, the fulfillment...*sets directly* before us, or at least more directly than the intention does. In fulfillment our experience is represented by the words: "This is the thing itself." (*LI,* 720)

We then encounter

varying amounts of intuitive fullness...which point...to possible gradients of fulfillment. Proceeding along these, we come to know the object better and better, by way of a presentative content that resembles it ever more and more clearly, and grasps it more and more vividly and fully. (*LI,* 745)

In each case of fulfillment, the properties of the object intended are grasped intuitively. Although a physical object can never be wholly present in intuition at one time, it stands as the ideal of complete fullness. But what can be known remains, for Husserl, what can be fully and clearly intuited.

Theory of fiction and transcendence

The theory of fiction that would issue from a phenomenological analysis of cinematic representation is able to take into account central cases. The long take from *Touch of Evil* will once again be illustrative. The picture that the hyperrealist theory of Bazin seems to convey is that important qualities of the object before the camera are preserved by photography so that the object of our experience of a motion picture has the same qualities (hence the analogies with decals). If so, it may seem that the actor/actress performances before the camera that night in Venice, California (where the long take was shot), are the objects conveyed to our experience by the automatic reproducibility of photography. It is, however, obvious that it is the bombing at the Mexican–American border that Bazin would want to be the object represented. Putting so much weight on automatic reproducibility, as Bazin does, with mediation in the process of apprehension *unacknowledged,* makes it seem that the acting performances are the objects experienced; meanwhile, the bombing, the fictional event, should be the object represented.

Transcendence theory would have no such problem with accounting for the fiction involved. With an acknowledgment of the complex mediation involved in apprehending the event portrayed – the bombing – transcendence theory has no difficulty in positing the bombing as *the* object represented. Fictional events, like real events, exist independently of perceivers' acts of apprehending them. Charlton Heston plays Vargas; Janet Leigh plays his wife, Suzie; Orson Welles plays Hank Quinlan. In experiencing *Touch of Evil* and its opening sequences, perceivers are constrained to apprehend the bombing, the relationship between Vargas and Suzie, the first appearances of Quinlan at the aftermath of the bombing, and so forth. They could focus on the Heston/Leigh/Welles performances as they could focus on camera position/camera movement/camera angle, but in apprehending what the opening sequences portray, they *pass through* performance and cinematic features to grasp that a bombing and its aftermath are *the* objects portrayed.

Spectatorship does not involve constructing the bombing out of the sensa to which the audience is exposed. That the event portrayed is fictional does not in any way require that its nature and existence be relative to the acts of the knowing mind experiencing it. One cannot attentively experience the opening sequences of the film, engage in the act of grasping what is represented, but yet also have a choice in finding not the bombing event but some other event portrayed (although interpretations of the event may vary), another one constructed out of the images and sounds. The bombing is, of course, a large event composed of many smaller events – setting the bomb, Linacre and his girlfriend riding in the car with the bomb to the border, Vargas and Suzie walking to the border nearby to the car, the car crossing the border, the kiss, the explosion. It is a commonplace that an event is composed of smaller events.

In apprehending the bombing at the border, perceivers are subjected to a large number of sensa – images and sounds – that constrain their intending of *the* object represented. Perceivers intending is also constrained by relevant horizons governing features of the intended object. The noemata that are formed are codetermined by awareness of hyletic data and the horizons brought to bear by perceivers. These noemata are apperceived as a moment in the process that succeeds in apprehending the bombing as the object represented. The fictional event – the bombing – is the object perceivers intuit. As such, fulfillment has obtained. It may seem that there is an inconsistency in making intuition the locus of apprehension. If intuition is direct apprehension of the object, how can there be a complex process of mediation involved in such apprehension? Apprehension of the bombing at the border is founded on *apperception* of noemata that constrain that apprehension:

It is *not* founded on *perception* of any other object (*LI*, 787ff). Apperception of the noemata arises together with perception of the border bombing as a moment in the process, a relationship that renders the act intuitive.

The examples of *Touch of Evil* do not bias the analysis in favor of a phenomenological account of representation. In any instance of spectators apprehending cinematic representations, no matter how bravura the style, no matter how many ellipses are employed, no matter how much presence of the process of inscription is made evident, intuition is the disposition or faculty spectators employ in knowing the representations in a motion picture.

The Oshima oeuvre analyzed in the previous section has all the ellipses, self-reflexivity, and exposure of the underlying ideology that any one would ever want in a motion picture experience. Nevertheless, in all of the representation in a film such as *Boy* or *The Ceremony* (*Gishiki*), or even in as radically dislocating a film as *Night and Fog in Japan*, spectators' apprehension of what is depicted, portrayed, or symbolized is accomplished by means of intuition with transcendence marking the perceptual process.

Night and Fog in Japan was inspired by Resnais's *Night and Fog* (*Nuit et Brouillard*) a 1955 documentary on the Nazi concentration camps. Oshima's focus is the failure of the Japanese student movement surrounding the issue of whether to ratify AMPO, the security treaty between Japan and the United States that, if adopted, ensured continuance of the American presence in Japan. The student movement ultimately failed to achieve abrogation of the security treaty primarily because of a failure within the resistance movement itself. Oshima blamed

those who possessed the qualities of leadership yet failed to utilize them, abstaining from the struggle, those who, having once faced up to the struggle, were disheartened by setbacks and those who secretly harbored pleasure in the chaos for its own sake.[12]

In the film, Oshima occasionally reverts to some of the most abstract moments one could imagine in a film portraying an event. Characters are spotlighted in shallow focus against a black background. Cinema transforms, as it were, into theater in sequences that ostensibly portray a wedding between a journalist, guilty over his abstention from the struggle against AMPO, and Reiko, a much younger woman who is a member of the New Left who has been involved in the protests. A wedding may seem the most personal of ceremonies, but the engulfing political struggle takes center stage.

The wedding takes place after AMPO has been ratified. The militants explore why their resistance efforts have failed. The movement of the film from cinematic texture to that of theater is striking. It serves to position the audience at critical distance toward the AMPO resistance, which might have been difficult, given the deep feelings of all those involved in this revolutionary movement. That there occurs a sudden assimilation in manner of representation to that of the theater and a movement away from what has come to be associated with cinematic expression in no way calls into question the phenomenological account of the spectator as discoverer of what is being depicted and portrayed using intuition as a means of accessing the representation. We know that this manner of representation is being used to embody a critique and position a productive critical distance toward AMPO resistance. The strategy requires extreme spectator activity; horizon governing theatrical representation govern the codetermination of the noemata in a way they usually do not in cinematic experience. But if spectators apprehend the internal critique of the AMPO movement and respond to the challenge to be positioned critically toward it, their intuitive grasp of the representations is in no way attenuated, to be replaced by some constructive activity, faculty, or disposition. If spectators know the film's representations, they know them intuitively, they codetermine mediating noemata, and their consciousness is intentional/transcendent.

Husserl has provided the method of reduction for examining the nature of such experiences. When we look within the experience of a radically decentering film such as *Night and Fog in Japan*, we find apperception and perception to be at work; we find transcendent events; we find the noemata/noeses involved. Moreover, reflection on what the nature of systematic codes must be – in the presence of a total relevance factor governing apprehension of complex portrayal subjects in cinematic experience – should convince us that the abrupt shift from cinematic to theatrical texture in the wedding sequence involves no spectator imposition of codes. It is only the attractiveness of the idealist/nominalist concept that would make the abrupt shifts from the cinematic to the theatrical seem a counterinstance. Only if one believes that perception stops with images and sounds does the abrupt shifts to theatrical rendering in the Oshima film seem to offer counterinstance to the transcendence theory of cinematic representation. Whether the objects represented are fictional or real, whether they are rendered in a primarily cinematic or theatrical way, whether they position us productively or not, transcendence is essential to the process of knowing cinematic representations.

Thus, transcendence theory of cinematic representation can give an account of fiction in a way that alternative accounts – transparency and transactional[13] – cannot. It highlights the intuitive richness of the experience of representation, it acknowledges the highly mediating role that consciousness plays, while establishing the grounds for the independent existence of the objects represented, whether they be fictional or real.

Husserl's epistemology as told by Jean-Louis Baudry

Jean-Louis Baudry's essay "Ideological Effects of the Basic Cinematographic Apparatus"[1] has had much influence on the direction in which film theory has developed. In support of his view about the nature of the cinematic apparatus and cinematic representation, Baudry makes reference to Husserl's epistemological theory; his reading of Husserl is, however, mistaken with ramifications for the fruitfulness of his conceptualizations of the nature of cinematic representation.

Baudry identifies different modes of representation. In one mode, the subject is "the active center and origin of meaning" (IE, 532). Baudry wishes us to be aware of the role that the cinematic apparatus plays in constituting representations:

We must first establish the place of the instrumental base in the set of operations which combine in the production of a film. . . . Between "objective reality" and the camera, site of the inscription and projection, are situated certain operations, a *work* which has as its results a finished product. (IE, 533)

Baudry then claims that there is an extent to which this product is cut off from the raw material, which he identifies with objective reality; this product, the film, "does not allow us to see the transformation which has taken place" (IE, 533). There follow various contentions about the work process culminating in the product. The camera occupies an intermediate position in the work process between objective reality and the product, contributing to the hiding of the work process. Decoupage and montage operate on script (language) and images (visuals), respectively, both of which are best thought of as signifying material. Projection and screen are also interventions. Their dual operations introduce "an unrolling," a transformation of a succession of separate images restoring "the movement seized from objective reality" (IE, 533).

Baudry invokes an Althusserian perspective in asking whether a "knowledge effect" is produced or if the work of the apparatus is concealed (IE, 533). Baudry's view is that the transformations effected by the work of the apparatus is concealed by the practices of the dominant cinema (IE, 533–4). If, on the other hand, cinema were to reveal the marks of its own inscription, a knowledge effect could obtain, which would serve as denunciation of and resistance to the dominant ideology.

Baudry follows with an argument to the effect that Renaissance per-spective construction has served as a model for dominant cinema, pro-ducing a centering effect, with the subject at the center of the space so constituted (IE, 534). Baudry discusses illusions that result from the operations of the apparatus. Though the subject is "really" experienc-ing only a series of images with no movement in them, the rapidity of their projection gives the illusion of movement:

The projection operation (projector and screen) restore continuity of movement and the temporal dimension to the sequence of static images. (IE, 535)

He goes on to explain that the working of persistence of vision in cre-ating the illusion of movement can operate only on condition that there be an effacement of differences (discontinuous elements, sepa-rate frames, there being only images). Baudry wants to contend that the illusion of representation in cinema is similarly based on using the potentials and limitations of the cinematic apparatus while simul-taneously concealing its use. That we really experience only individual images is suppressed so that representations may appear without cin-ematic strategies being utilized, which will reveal this transformation and illusion-making activity.

Baudry links his analysis of the illusion of movement with an analy-sis of spectatorship under the influence of the operations of the cine-matic apparatus. The apparatus creates the illusion of movement where there is none. For the subject

to seize movement is to become movement, to follow a trajectory is to become a trajectory, . . . to determine a meaning is to give oneself a meaning. (IE, 536–7)

Baudry is moving toward the view that "the moveability of the camera seems to fulfill the most favorable conditions for the manifestation of the transcendental subject" (IE, 537). As such, there is both a fantas-matization of an objective reality and an augmenting of the powers of the subject (IE, 537).

It is at this point that Baudry refers to and quotes Husserl in order to support his views on the nature of the subject. Baudry first utilizes Husserl's doctrine of intentionality – that consciousness is always consciousness of something – which as we have seen entails that the object of consciousness exists independently. Baudry puts the doctrine in the following way: "the image will always be an image *of* some-thing; it must result from a deliberate act of consciousness" (IE, 537). Then he quotes Husserl from the *Cartesian Meditations* as follows:

The word intentionality signifies nothing other than this peculiarity that consciousness has of being consciousness of something, of carrying in its qualities of ego, its cogitatum within itself.[2]

In this Husserlian passage, *cogitationes* are acts of cognition and *cogitatum* is the object cognized. Baudry interprets Husserl to mean the following:

In such a definition could perhaps be found the status of the cinematographic image, or rather of its operation, the mode of working which it carries out. For it to be an image of something, it has to constitute this something as meaning. The image seems to reflect the world but solely in the naive inversion of a founding hierarchy. (IE, 537)

Baudry is drawing an analogy between the operation of consciousness as described by Husserl and the operation of the cinematic apparatus as well as the status of the image. He is claiming that for an image to be an image of something, to be intentional in Husserl's sense, "[the image] has to constitute [its object] as meaning." He must be contending that the image has the power to constitute a property of an object or give meaning to an object while at the same time being constituted itself by the operation of the cinematic apparatus. If American society in midcentury is the object symbolized by Welles's *Citizen Kane,* and a shot of Orson Welles playing Charles Foster Kane is the image, the shot constitutes the fictional character, Kane, and constitutes the American society, while also being constituted by all of the phases of the cinematic apparatus at work.

The image thereby has extraordinary powers. For instance, there is the famous shot of gubernatorial candidate Kane in an upward angle with a huge poster of his likeness behind him. This image creates or contributes to the creation of Kane and contributes to constituting midcentury American society or its soul. For it to be an image of either, moreover, it must constitute them in some such way.

We have seen that Husserl wants intentionality to work just the other way around. The objects represented by art exist independently of the intentional act of apprehending them. If midcentury American society or its soul is symbolized or William Randolph Hearst is parodied or a fictional character Charles Foster Kane is portrayed by the image(s) of *Citizen Kane,* Husserl will not serve as support for a view that the image constitutes these symbolized, parodied, or portrayed objects. Husserl wants representation to guide our perception to its independently existing object. Baudry leaves out the dual operations of the noema/noesis in the constitution of meaning. It is with respect to the noema that meaning becomes constituted; the something referred to in the preceding quote is not constituted by consciousness. The noema must be part of any analysis of Husserlian theory, but Baudry is leaving this vital dimension out of the analysis.

To further support his interpretation that for Husserl the meaning of an object is constituted by the subject, Baudry quotes the following passage from *Cartesian Meditations:*

The domain of natural existence thus has only an authority of the second order, and always presupposes the domain of the transcendental. (*CM*, 21)

For Husserl, the domain of natural existence is the domain of things as regarded from the natural standpoint. Husserl is making the observation that the domain of natural existence presupposes, in its essence, consciousness adopting the natural standpoint. This consciousness exists independently of the act of consciousness. He is not saying anything that can be used to justify the view that representations in a work of art are constituted by the subject.

Baudry believes, however, that he has shown that Husserlian phenomenology will support his idealist epistemology. Again passing over the distinction between the noema and *the* object represented by the film, he offers the following analysis:

Limited by the framing, lined up, put at the proper distance, the world offers up an object, implied by and implying the action of the "subject" which sights it. At the same time, the world's transfer as image seems to accomplish this phenomenological reduction, this putting into parentheses of its real existence (a suspension necessary . . . to the formation of the impression of reality). (IE, 537)

The connection that Baudry seeks to make between the cinematic apparatus transforming the world into image and the phenomenological reduction will not hold up. As we have seen, to perform the reduction has nothing to do with changing the nature of *The* object of perception. It is a method for becoming aware of the relationship between subject and object as the noema/noesis obtain. The object remains the same throughout the reduction: When we bracket, we put aside our natural standpoint assumptions and become aware of the manner of codetermination of the noema by subject and object. It will not do for Baudry to try to make it look as if Husserl can justify putting aside the referent in analyzing cinematic representation.

Baudry then turns his attention to the subject in the experience of representation. Husserl is enlisted to justify the claim that meanings of objects have their locus in the activity of the subject, not in being properties of objects existing independently of the subject's activity. He quotes further from *Cartesian Meditations:*

The original operation [of intentional analysis] is to mask the potentialities implied in present states of consciousness. And it is by this that will be carried out, from the noematic point of view, the eventual explication, definition, and elucidation of what is meant by consciousness, that is, its objective meaning. (*CM*, 46)

Baudry then quotes a passage about the nature of this consciousness:

A second type of polarization now presents itself to us, another type of synthesis which embraces the particular multiplicities of cogitationes, which embraces them all and in a special manner, namely, as cogitationes of an identical self which, active or passive, lives in all the lived states of consciousness and which, through them, relates to all objects. (*CM*, 66)

Baudry argues that for Husserl,

the multiplicity of aspects of the object in view refers to a synthesizing operation, to the unity of this constituting subject. Husserl speaks of aspects...the consciousness of which though it remain unperceived, always accompanies them. (IE, 537)

Each aspect that the mind grasps is revealed in turn as a unity synthesized from a multiplicity of corresponding modes of presentation.

Baudry is not explaining what "noematic" means in the first of these passages. Had he understood what the noema is in the Husserlian system, he would have realized that Husserl is, in these passages, marking the codetermination of the noema; it is not the case that an attribute such as continuity in the object is constructed in the object by the perceiver. Nevertheless, Baudry's interpretation of these passages is as follows:

Thus is articulated the relation between the continuity necessary to the constitution of meaning and the subject which constitutes this meaning: continuity is an attribute of the subject. (IE, 538)

Husserl speaks of the object represented in the Dürer engraving as a "flesh and blood knight" specifically to foreclose against any such interpretation of representation. If there is continuity in the film, it is a feature discovered by the subject via guidance to that recognition by the noema/noesis, which consciousness codetermines. The self exists independently of its perceptual acts according to Husserl. As it operates, it is not the object of perception, though its presence in the perceptual process is apperceived; if the reduction is performed, its presence as codeterminer of the noema can be recognized.

Believing that Husserl has provided support for his theory about the relationship of the cinematic apparatus to the constitution of representations, Baudry proceeds to elaborate his account. He wants to argue that

the search for...narrative continuity, so difficult to obtain from the material base, can only be explained by an essential ideological stake projected in this point: it is a question of preserving at any cost the synthetic unity of the locus where meaning originates (the subject) – the constituting transcendental function to which narrative continuity point back as its natural secretion. (IE, 538)

We have seen that Baudry can neither justify reading such an idealist view about representation into Husserl nor derive support for it from his phenomenological system.

Notes

Husserl's theory of artistic representation

1. In understanding Husserl's theory, it is important to compare and contrast the translations of *Ideas* by Kersten and Gibson. In this passage, I substitute "turn attention to" for Kersten's "advert."

2. Bill Nichols, *Ideology and the Image: Social Representation in Cinema and Other Media* (Bloomington: Indiana University Press, 1981), pp. 35–6.

3. Ibid., pp. 11–12.

4. For references to the noema and noesis in *Ideas* see the analytic index to the Gibson translation (esp. §§85b, 88b). For a richer understanding of the noema and related notions, see Appendix A of that work.

5. On the term *sensa* see C. D. Broad, *The Mind and Its Place in Nature* (Patterson, N.J.: Littlefield, Adams & Co., 1960), pp. 180–3.

6. *LI*, I§23. See also Dallas Willard, *Logic and the Objectivity of Knowledge: A Study in Husserl's Early Philosophy* (Athens: Ohio University Press, 1984), p. 80, n. 43 for a most useful discussion of the nature of apperception in Husserl and the way in which the term *apperception* was used in the philosophical milieu in which Husserl wrote.

7. Nichols, *Ideology and the Image*, p. 240.

8. Francis Russell, *The World of Dürer: 1471–1528* (New York: Time, Inc., 1967), pp. 58–9.

9. On codetermination of the noemata by the perceiver, see Husserl's *Experiences and Judgment* (hereafter *EJ*), §83a and *Cartesian Meditations* (hereafter *CM*), §22.

10. On the constructionist approach in contemporary film theory, see J. Dudley Andrew, *Concepts in Film Theory* (Oxford: Oxford University Press, 1985), chaps. 5 and 8.

11. On the concept of horizon in Husserl, see David Woodruff Smith and Ronald McIntyre, *Husserl and Intentionality: A Study of Mind, Meaning, and Language* (Dordrecht [The Netherlands] and Boston: Reidel, 1982), chap. V. There they explain horizon as well as point to the many discussions in several Husserl texts of horizon. For a discussion of the application of horizon to literary theory, see E. D. Hirsch, *Validity in Interpretation* (New Haven: Yale University Press, 1967), appendix IA, "Two Horizons of Textual Meaning."

The concept of the noema

1. David Woodruff Smith and Ronald McIntyre, *Husserl and Intentionality: A Study of Mind, Meaning, and Language* (Dordrecht [The Netherlands] and Boston: Reidel, 1982), chaps. 3 and 4.

2. Martin Heidegger, *Being and Time*, trans. J. MacQuarrie and E. Robinson (New York: Harper & Row, 1962), p. 51. Hereafter abbreviated as *BT*.

3. Plato, *Republic*, trans. Benjamin Jowett, in *Plato's Dialogues* (Oxford: Clarendon Press, 1953).

4. All quotations in this and the next paragraph are from *BT*, 51.

5. These three quotations are from *BT*, 52.

·6. *BT*, 51–2; see note 1.

7. Quotations are from *BT*, 53.

8. Dallas Willard, "Historical and Philosophical Foundation of Phenomenology," unpublished paper, p. 22.

9. For example, *I*, §97, 261; §98, 264 (pages refer to the 1962 ed.).

10. H. Cornelius, *Versuch einer Theory der Existentialurteile* (Munich: Riegersche Universitats Buchhandlund, 1894).

11. See *Husserliana* (hereafter *H*) *XXII*, p. 374.

12. For alternative accounts of the noema, see Aron Gurwitsch, *The Field of Consciousness* (Pittsburgh: Duquesne University Press, 1964); Dagfinn Follesdal, "Husserl's Notion of Noema," *Journal of Philosophy*, 66 (1969), 680–7.

The ontology of cinematic representation

1. On the distinction between nominalism and realism, see D. M. Armstrong, *Universals and Scientific Realism, Vol. 1, Nominalism and Realism* (New York: Cambridge University Press, 1980), chaps. 1 and 2.

2. Nelson Goodman's views about artistic representation are to be found in his *Languages of Art* (Indianapolis: Hackett Publishing, 1968).

3. Quotations are from J. Dudley Andrew, *Concepts in Film Theory* (Oxford, Oxford University Press, 1984), p. 38.

4. Goodman, *Languages of Art*, p. 6.

5. Ibid.

6. Ibid., pp. 36–7.

7. Ibid., p. 6.

8. Søren Kjørup, "Film as a Meetingplace of Multiple Codes," in David Perkins and Barbara Leondar, eds., *The Arts and Cognition* (Baltimore and London: Johns Hopkins Press, 1977), p. 31.

9. Ibid.

10. Andrew, *Concepts in Film Theory*, p. 48.

11. Ibid.

12. Ibid., pp. 48–9.
13. Roland Barthes, *Critique et Vérité* (Paris: Editions de Seuil, 1968).
14. Noel Carroll, "The Power of the Movies," *Daedalus* (Fall 1985), p. 83.
15. *LI II*, chaps. 2 and 3, 350–74.
16. D. M. Armstrong, *Nominalism and Realism*, p. 11.
17. Ibid., p. 12.
18. Ibid.
19. Ibid., p. 19.
20. Ibid.
21. Ibid., p. xiii.
22. Ibid., p. 12.
23. Ibid.
24. Ibid., p. 16.
25. On predicate nominalism, see Armstrong, *Nominalism and Realism*, p. 13; on concept nominalism, see Armstrong, p. 25.

The epistemology of cinematic representation

1. Maureen Turim and John Mowitt, "Thirty Seconds over...Oshima's *The War of Tokyo or The Young Man Who Left His Will on Film*," *Wide Angle*, 1(4) (1977).
2. Ibid.
3. Ibid., p. 35.
4. Paul Coates, "Repetition and Contradiction in the Films of Oshima," *Quarterly Review of Film and Video*, 11 (1990), 65–71.
5. Dana Polan, "Politics as Process in Three Films by Nagisa Oshima," *Film Criticism*, 8 (1) (Fall 1983), 34.
6. Ibid.
7. Ibid., p. 36
8. Peter Wollen, *Signs and Meaning in the Cinema*, 3rd ed. conclusion (Bloomington: Indiana University Press, 1972), p. 161.
9. Edward Branigan, "Subjectivity under Siege – From Fellini's *8½* to Oshima's *The Story of the Man Who Left His Will on Film*," *Screen*, 19(1) (1978), 27. See Joan Mellen, *Waves at Genji's Door: Japan Through Its Films* (New York: Pantheon, 1976), p. 369, for a similar idea about *He Died after the War*.
10. Christian Metz, *Language and Cinema*, trans. Donna Jean Uniker-Seabock (The Hague: Mouton, 1974), chap. VI, p. 3, and Christian Metz, *The Imaginary Signifier: Psychoanalysis and the Cinema*, trans. by Celia Britton, Annwyl Williams, Ben Brewster, and Alfred Guzzetti (Bloomington: Indiana University Press, 1982), p. 36.
11. Wollen, *Signs and Meaning*, p. 162.
12. J. Dudley Andrew, *Concepts in Film Theory* (Oxford: Oxford University Press, 1985), see p. 91 on the notion of the bourgeois realist text, that media product that is offered to spectators "complete" in itself, neither invites nor rewards spectator investment.
13. Roland Barthes, *S/Z* (Boston: Hill & Wang, 1974), pp. 3–5.
14. Turim and Mowitt, "Thirty Seconds," 35.
15. Stephen Heath, "The Question Oshima," *Wide Angle*, 2(1) (1977), 53. See

also Peter Lehman's, "The Avant-garde: Power, Change, and the Power to Change," in *Cinema Histories, Cinema Practices,* ed. by P. Mellencamp and P. Rosen, AFI Monograph Series (Frederick, Md.: University Publications of America, 1984), pp. 120–9.

16. Heath, "The Question Oshima," 53.
17. Branigan, "Subjectivity under Siege," 29.
18. Ibid.
19. Ibid. See also Paul Willemen, "Notes on Subjectivity: On Reading Edward Branigan's Subjectivity under Siege," *Screen,* 19(1) (Spring 1978), 41–69 for a criticism of Branigan's position and see Branigan's reply, "Foreground and Background: A Reply to Paul Willemen," *Screen,* 19(2) (Summer 1978), 135–40.
20. See Willard van Orman Quine, *Philosophy of Logic* (Englewood Cliffs, N.J.: Prentice-Hall, 1970), p. 81.
21. G. A. Cohen, *Karl Marx's Theory of History: A Defense* (Princeton: Princeton University Press, 1978), p. 297.
22. Coates, "Repetition and Contradiction."
23. Wollen, *Signs and Meaning,* conclusion, p. 161.
24. Ibid., p. 163.
25. For an elaboration of this analysis, see Allan Casebier, "A Presentational Model for Aesthetic Verdicts," *British Journal of Esthetics,* 24(2) (Spring 1984), 113–15.
26. Arnold Isenberg, "Critical Communication," *Philosophical Review,* LVIII (1949), 330–44; reprinted in John Hospers, *Introductory Readings in Aesthetics* (New York: Free Press, 1969), p. 261.
27. David Bordwell, *Narration in the Fiction Film* (Madison: University of Wisconsin Press, 1985), chaps. 9, 10, and 12.

Transaction, transparency, and transcendence

1. André Bazin, *What Is Cinema? Vol. I,* trans. Hugh Gray (Berkeley: University of California Press, 1967), p. 28.
2. Ibid., p. 14.
3. Ibid., p. 15.
4. Ibid., p. 13.
5. Ibid., p. 15. Kendall Walton in "Transparent Pictures," *Critical Inquiry,* II (2) (December 1984), and in "Looking Again Through Photographs," *Critical Inquiry,* 12 (Summer 1986), has presented a most challenging version of the transparency thesis for photography. Walton contends that when we look at a photograph of our dead grandfather, we *literally see* the dead grandfather with the assistance of photography.
6. Bazin, "Evolution of the Film Language," *What Is Cinema? Vol. I.*
7. Bazin, "Ontology of the Film Image," *What Is Cinema? Vol. I.*
8. Bazin, "de Sica: Metteur en Scene," *What Is Cinema? Vol. II,* trans. Hugh Gray (Berkeley: University of California Press, 1971).
9. Bazin, "An Aesthetic of Reality," *What Is Cinema? Vol. II.*
10. For explication of Stanley Cavell's version of the transparency theory, and Alexander Sesonske's criticism of it (upon which I could not improve), see

Stanley Cavell, *The World Viewed: Enlarged Edition* (Cambridge, Mass.: Harvard University Press, 1979). Cavell responds to Sesonske's criticisms on pp. 162–230.

11. Edmund Husserl, "Psychological Studies in the Elements of Logic" (hereafter PS), p. 304.

12. From the script for *Night and Fog in Japan*, trans. Keiko Mochizuki; cited in Joan Mellen, *Waves at Genji's Door: Japan Through Its Films* (New York: Pantheon, 1976).

13. For a transactional analysis of *Touch of Evil*, see Stephen Heath, "Film and System: Terms of Analysis, Part I," *Screen*, 16 (1975–6), 7–51.

Husserl's epistemology as told by Jean-Louis Baudry

1. Jean-Louis Baudry, "Ideological Effects of the Basic Cinematographic Apparatus," in Bill Nichols, *Movies and Methods, Vol. II* (Berkeley: University of California Press, 1985), pp. 531–42; hereafter abbreviated as IE. All quotes from this work are © 1974 by the Regents of the University of California, and reprinted from *Film Quarterly*, 28(2) (Winter 1974–5), 39–47, where Baudry's article first appeared.

2. The quote is from Edmund Husserl, *Les meditations Cartesiennes* (Paris: Vrin, 1953), 28. The English translation is *Cartesian Meditations: An Introduction to Phenomenology*, trans. Dorion Cairns (The Hague: Nijhoff, 1960). However, Baudry used the French original in his discussion.

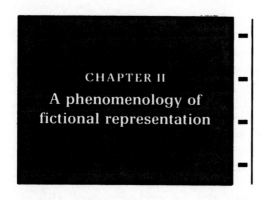

CHAPTER II

A phenomenology of fictional representation

Without realizing the ontological and epistemological difficulties involved in its nominalist and idealist roots, and without knowing of the viability of realist alternatives, contemporary film theory has attempted to answer some of the questions about cinematic representation by looking for and utilizing idealist/nominalist frameworks. Had realist frameworks been employed, the accounts would have been different, and there are reasons to think they would have been better.

This chapter will be devoted to a delineation of the advantages of a phenomenological model for fictional representations in film over its prevailing contemporary counterpart. The seeking out of a concept compatible with the idealist/nominalist framework rather than the realist may be found in a number of the main activities of contemporary film theory: theorizing the relationships between Western and Eastern styles of representation, pinpointing the interactions among sound and image in film experience, conceptualizing the relation of narrative and the world of the work, explaining the unities found in cinematic representations, and developing a theory of portrayal of women in film. In the search for the idealist/nominalist concept, contemporary film theory has posited some unnecessary entities, as we shall see, including the fantasmatic body, the fabula, the diegesis, and the Imaginary.

An oriental mode of cinematic representation

In his highly influential inquiry into the Japanese cinema, *To the Distant Observer*,[1] Noel Burch argues for the view that at its best, cinematic depiction, portrayal, and symbolism in Japanese cinema has been "presentational" not "representational" in particular senses of these terms. Burch's study is especially significant to examine in that it calls into question the value of representation itself. It will become apparent that idealism/nominalism are unquestioned assumptions guiding Burch's analysis.

83

Burch utilizes several interrelated concepts in identifying a distinctively Japanese mode of cinematic expression. The Japanese aesthetic approach, according to Burch, is presentational whereas its Western counterpart is representational (*TDO,* 69–72). By this contrast he means that the Japanese art object emphasizes its being a presentation rather than serving to represent something external to itself. For instance, when we experience a Bunraku doll theater performance, the puppeteers are revealed to the audience throughout the performance whereas in the West concealment is the prevailing mode.

Thus, when we watch a Bunraku play, we are confronted with an *opaque* rather than a transparent surface. That is, we do not "look through" the actions on the stage to grasp a world of objects, persons, and events existing independently of the performance; instead the content of consciousness is surface, that is a condition where signifier is divorced from the signified.

Burch quotes Roland Barthes's account of the Bunraku: The doll theater practices three separate modes of writing – the effective gesture of the doll, the affecting gesture of the puppeteer, and the vocal gesture of the narrator (*TDO,* 73).

Presentational mode may be recognized in Heian poetry where we encounter *Kakekotoba* (pivot word form),

a rhetorical scheme of word-play in which a series of sounds is so employed as to mean two or more things at once by different parsings. (*TDO,* 47)

This feature of Japanese literature shows the extent to which the Japanese mind rejects linearity and the transparency of the signifier, which has dominated both Western thought and art since the eighteenth century (*TDO,* 47).

The Kabuki theater also tends to reveal the inscription of textural production via the visibility of the *koroko* (the stagehands) and the musicians (*TDO,* 68–9). The upshot is that in the West the processes that create illusion are concealed in ways that are made apparent to the spectator of Japanese art. In a related feature, in the Japanese case the narrative elements are separated from other aspects of the production while in the Western case, the narrative elements are inextricably bound up with every other part. For example, in Kabuki, the actors do not speak the words, chanters do so, with musicians providing still a third, independent element (*TDO,* 70).

The modes of representation that Burch isolates in this process of comparing East and West are ideologically charged. The West has an ideology of representation "suited to the needs of the bourgeoise. ... The masking of the process of the production of meaning became as important, on its own level, as that of the process of production of goods. This ideology continues to dominate our [Western] notions of representations to this day" (*TDO*, 47).

The same is true for the film. The ideology of the transparency of the sign dominated the emergence of the Western film from its primitive stage whereas the inscription of the signifying process in the text was the primary influence in the development of Japanese cinema in the twentieth century (*TDO*, 47). Accordingly, sections in *To the Distant Observer* are devoted to showing how Kinugasa, Ozu, Mizoguchi, Naruse, and others in the golden age of Japanese cinema (the late 1920s and 1930s) developed a cinema that was presentational: opaque rather than transparent (*TDO*, 113), decentered rather than centered (*TDO*, 85, 116, 157). We have discussed the opaque versus transparent dichotomy. The practice of continuity editing, especially in terms of eyeline matching (*TDO*, 159–60), receives special attention in Burch in a way related to the centered–decentered distinction. The centered–decentered distinction has to do with spectator positioning. When centered, the audience has the sense of the spectacle as existing for its perception and consumption. When decentered, the audience has no such sense. Continuity between shots, which has the characters' looks matching one another across cuts as they speak to one another or otherwise relate to one another, is identified by Burch as

the most crucial element of the Western editing system . . . it was this procedure which made it possible to implicate the spectator in the physical–mental space of the world of the film. (*TDO*, 158)

Such a procedure is regarded by Burch as "basic to the illusionist fantasy/identification situation" (*TDO*, 158). Since Ozu set up his camera so as to produce incorrect eyeline matches, he is applauded for having "challenged the dominant Western code of editing in which the viewer is included in the film situation as invisible, transparent relay in the communion of the two characters" (*TDO*, 159). The film becomes for the viewer, feeling himself an invisible relay, a spectacle made for his or her consumption, with the link to key notions such as bourgeois and illusionism apparent.

With the end of World War II, the American occupation, capitalism, and "democracy" come to Japan. According to Burch with them also comes the decline of the Japanese cinema. Instead of the cinema we knew in Japan's golden age of the 1930s, we have a cinema of capitulation, one that becomes assimilated to "the dominant codes" of cinematic representation. Late Ozu, late Mizoguchi, much of Kurosawa (e.g., *The Seven Samurai* [*Shichinin no samurai*]), much of what had been thought the greatness of Japanese cinema is put in "proper perspective" as degenerate expressions of capitalism via the use of techniques of bourgeois illusionism. The history of postwar Ozu is the history of "a gradual fossilization." Where Kurosawa is praised, it is because of his deconstruction of the dominant Hollywood codes of cinematic expression – that is, he took the Western mode and turned it back upon itself.

Burch's concern with cinema is, therefore, everywhere formal. He seeks differences in the forms that Japanese as opposed to Western filmmakers (and artists in general in the two cultures) utilized. His assumption is that if we describe Japanese cinema or cinema in the West (or if we evaluate) we need to identify the forms that each develops: ways of showing things not what is shown; ways of editing not what content is communicated; ways of positioning the spectator in relation to the film not what the film has to say or show us about the human condition. Always everything lines up neatly between the two cultures. In the West, because of the dominant style used, the viewer is positioned as a capitalist subject; in the 1930s cinema of Japan, the viewer is positioned in a critical state of mind where he or she is not made to feel absorbed in the fictional, illusionistic world of the film but rather is positioned in a state of mind compatible with critical apprehension of the filmic apparatus.

In order to focus the issues that Burch is developing, it will be useful to see how he analyzes the work of Japan's celebrated filmmaker, Akira Kurosawa. For Burch, a crucial framework for assessing the Japanese cinema in general and Kurosawa in particular is provided by the concept of the diegesis. The *diegesis* is conceptualized as the "fictional world of the film." As Burch puts it:

The diegesis is for instance the world of Balzac which his readers enter, those imagined drawing rooms . . . those imagined characters. (*TDO*, 18–19)

(More will be said about the concept of the diegesis in a later section of this chapter.) It has been the tendency of Western cinema, according to Burch, to create a cinematic practice that aims at absorbing spectators in the diegesis. Thus, Kurosawa is to be lauded for his removal of the spectator from his or her customary absorption in the diegesis and is criticized for those instances where his cinema maximizes the diegetic effect.

Kurosawa's "rough-hewn" geometry (*TDO*, 298) in some of his well-known films, such as *Rashomon,* comes in for special praise. In earlier films, Kurosawa had aimed at the organic form characteristic of the dominant Western cinema accompanied by the usual absorption in the diegesis and cultivation of a story sense of diegetic illusion. Elements in the rough-hewn geometry are use of the hard-edged wipe for transitions, the 180° reverse-angle cut and sharply contrasting (and frequent) juxtaposition (e.g., close-up and long shot), and moving and fixed shots. The effect of this approach is to expose the process of articulation, reveal the making of the diegetic illusion, which correspondingly inhibits the sense of strong diegetic illusion (*TDO*, 298).

On the other hand, Kurosawa is criticized for such stylistics as the way in which he "never in any way disrupts the unambiguous definition of spatial relations" (*TDO*, 299). Occasionally as in *Living* (*Ikiru*) there will be a mismatch that could, if coordinated with following shots, disclose the illusion-making character of the filmic-practice. Kurosawa, however, instantly resolves the mismatch in *Living* by placing both characters on the screen together, clarifying the spatial geography for the spectators before they have time to "see through" the illusion of cinematic making of space (*TDO*, 299); Kurosawa always adheres in an underlying way to Western linearity. As Burch puts it: "Ambiguity in Kurosawa ... is an element of tension to be answered by one of resolution ... never is it a categorical indifference to univalence or linearity as it is in Ozu" (*TDO*, 299). Kurosawa's manner involves combining signifying elements; for example, in *Living* in a content of "wholly unambiguous narrative claim," or Watanabe's progress from foreknowledge of death to the "petit bourgeois" realization that he can do something meaningful himself (*TDO*, 306).

Burch notes that even the most modest picture from Japan often displays a more or less systematically decentered composition (*TDO*, 306). When Kurosawa uses decentering as in *The Lower Depths* (*Donzoko*), he is praised; where he does not, he is criticized for his participation and furtherance of diegetic illusionism.

Burch concludes with a chilling assessment of Kurosawa:

It would seem that [the Japanese film industry's] stiflingly repressive structures have ultimately broken the one true master which the post-war Japanese cinema has known. (*TDO*, 321)

Burch is led to look back on the silent period in Japanese cinema as a golden age (*TDO*, 143); the cinematic apparatus was foregrounded, inhibiting diegetic illusionism and sensitizing the audience to the constructedness of all filmic articulation. The period in which Kurosawa gains international fame, the post–World War II era, is regarded by Burch as one in which Kurosawa (and others) compromised with Western-inspired diegetic illusionism.

In that earlier golden age of Japanese cinema, films bore the marks of their own inscription. For example, Ozu consistently mismatched conversations across cuts (*TDO*, 159); Kinugasa utilized presentational forms of exposition wherein the manner of presentation obtrudes upon spectator experience rendering the image opaque rather than transparent (*TDO*, 126–35); and so on.

However, with an understanding of (1) the distinction between perception and apperception and (2) recognition of the intentionality of representational consciousness, it may be seen that reflexivity is only one of the many ways in which cinematic experience may meaningfully occur. With representational consciousness transcending the mental acts involved in perception and founded on an apprehension of hyletic data and an apprehension of the noemata, representation per se does not become a feature of a film to be demeaned, as it does for Burch. If representation involves intentional apprehension of independently existing objects while images and sounds are only apperceived, judgments of value about a film should have their locus in the qualities of the objects grasped and their manner of exemplification not in an alleged spectator participation in or inhibition from an illusion-making activity.

Where Kurosawa represents events developing according to cause and effect in linear fashion, as in Watanabe's growth under the influence of an extreme situation (that is, foreknowledge of impending death) *in Living,* it is not a deficiency of the film that a part or all of it involves linearity. Rather than being properly described as diegetic illusionism, as Burch wants, this part of the film involves a transcendence to objects, events, and persons founded on apperception of hyletic data and noematic intentionality. That is, it is not that there are just images and sounds in our experience that, because of their proffered relationships, invite spectator construction of an illusion of reality. Objects of reality are apprehended in a way involving intentional transcendence, that is, feelings and emotions coincident with having foreknowledge of death.

In this light, the emphasis that Burch, in *To the Distant Observer,* places upon formal characteristics of Kurosawa films is misguided. The rough-hewn geometry serves the end of intentional transcendence, not the aim to disrupt absorption in the diegesis. Measuring the nature of cinematic representation in terms of how it *affects* spectators involves conflating two different relationships. In recognizing what a film represents, spectators engage in mental acts that are the proper locus for analyzing representation; it is quite another matter to isolate the affective relationships that occur coincident with an instance of representation. Indeed, a recognition of what a film depicts and/or portrays can occur in a context where there is no appreciable affective relation occurring.

The way Burch asks us to conceptualize the film experience biases the issue against Kurosawa. We are asked to accept the assumption that in the experience of a film such as *The Seven Samurai* there is only a set of images and sounds. As discussed earlier, such an assumption reflects the idealist/nominalist framework.* Such images would include shapes, volumes, movements, screen directions, camera position, sound texture, and so forth. These images may be presented to us in a way that will make us sensitive to *facture*,[2] the (supposed) constructedness of all filmic articulation, or they can be presented so as to cultivate absorption in the diegesis by hiding the constructedness and fostering our tendency to posit them as constituting a linear exemplification of events. The Husserlian notion of apperception directly counters this picture of the film experience, as noted earlier. We do not perceive volumes, sound textures, and so on; we perceive battles, rain, mud, alliances among villagers and samurai, and so forth. Moreover, it is not the case that facture marks all filmic expression. It is also not the case that various manners of presentation foster spectator construction of illusions of reality while others inhibit this tendency. Some films provide experiences in which objects of reality may be intentionally grasped by prepared observers (e.g., documentaries, a matter to be discussed in a later section); other films offer fictional events as their representational content (e.g., *The Seven Samurai*). Whether or not spectators become immersed in or distant from what has been called "the diegesis" carries no weight in analysis of cinematic representation.

The same may be said for the 180° reverse-field editing practice used by Kurosawa. It certainly has a different psychological affect on spectators than so-called invisible editing, wherein spectators may more easily form a sense of the geography of the action. It is, however, a non sequitur to conclude that the reverse-field editing will make the audience confront facture. The audience may simply have to deal with more complex hyletic data in being guided in their intentional grasp of the events and objects being portrayed. If, as in some avant-garde films, reverse-field editing practice is sustained over a lengthy portion of the film, articulation may well become the object of perception. But in the case of Kurosawa's use of this practice, it seems more likely that intentional apprehension of transcendent objects remains the content of perception, not a shift to images. As Burch notes, Kurosawa moves rather quickly in instances of reverse-field editing to reinstate a coherent geography. It seems much more likely that Kurosawa is aiming to foster audience transcendence to fictional events than to cultivate a vivid sense of facture. From this, it is apparent that Burch's criticism of Kurosawa rests on the idealist/nominalist framework, thereby reflect-

* Burch's section entitled "Some Terminological Indicators" (*TDO*, p. 18) is clearly idealist/nominalist. Burch says, for example, that "a referent is that which refers a linguistic sign to extra-linguistic referent as it has been articulated by a human group."

ing a failure to appreciate that there is a viable realist framework that may support a very different assessment of Kurosawa's work.

In addition, the distinction between representation and presentation so central to Burch's theory of the Japanese cinema, can only be made out against the background of the idealist/nominalist framework, and it is at odds with a phenomenology of the film experience of Japanese cinema.

Supposedly, when a picture (still or moving) is opaque, one cannot look through it; by contrast, when a picture is transparent, it is possible to look through it to see a world of objects, persons, and events. In the cases Burch cites – Bunraku, Kabuki, Ozu films of the golden age – the spectator apprehends objects, persons, and events despite the fact that there is the so-called inscription of the signifying process. In Bunraku, we *are* aware of the puppeteers manipulating the puppets in a way we usually are not in Western puppet theater. This awareness, however, does not prevent our perceiving action, objects, characters, and events in Chikamatsu's celebrated Bunraku play *Double Suicide*. When Shinoda makes his adaptation of *Double Suicide* (*Shinju ten no Amijima*) in 1969, he begins the film with a scene backstage at the Bunraku theater where he gives instructions to his scriptwriter about a scene in the graveyard. The parallel between the dolls manipulated by puppeteers and humans in the story manipulated by fate is made salient for the audience. Though there is a focus on the process of production in the Shinoda adaptation, it does not impede the audience's apprehension of the fictional world of the film.

If the metaphor of opaque and transparent were useful, we ought to have as the content of our consciousness the process of production not the story of the doomed lovers in both the Chikamatsu Bunraku original and in the Shinoda adaptation. The phenomenological facts are that the two awarenesses *arise together*, the one not impeding the other. To be sure, without the reflexive aspect provided by Shinoda, the audience awareness would be different. The audience seeks to make a connection between the "human story" and the "puppet story," between the content of the film and the reflexive aspect (Shinoda telling his scriptwriter what he wants in the very film we are seeing). However, the audience has just as *representationally rich* a world of objects, persons, and events to perceive as they would have without the reflexive dimension. We apprehend the relationship between the doomed couple, the woman's status as a prostitute, his wish to buy her freedom, the social obstacles that they face in pursuing the relationship, the complications involving the man's wife, the double suicide at the end, and so forth.

What Burch wants to call "presentation" functions on another continuum from representation, a continuum having to do with the manner of representation. Some depictions and some portrayals of objects are given to the audience without an accompanying awareness of the process of production. Others, such as the ones Burch cites, do come with this accompanying awareness. The depiction/portrayal subjects are the same regardless of the presence of the accompaniment. The opposite of presentation is hiding the work of the art. The opposite of representation is nonrepresentation. Nothing about golden age Japanese cinema or nouvelle vague Japanese cinema, such as that of Shinoda, precludes an experience of these films being both presentational and representational at the same time.

Thus, the effort to identify a distinctively oriental mode of cinematic representation rests upon a series of distinctions that cannot be justified. Given that the notion of such a mode derives from the perturbing idealist/nominalist framework, it should be clear that we have another reason for needing a realist analysis in understanding the nature of cinematic representation.

Cinematic sound

After neglecting cinematic sound in favor of the development of theories about the visual nature of cinema, theoretical writing about the nature of the motion picture has finally given it a thoroughgoing treatment. Weis and Belton's anthology *Film Sound: Theory and Practice*[1] presents several of the major writings about the relationship between visuals and sound in cinema. Two texts from this collection will be indicative of the direction that such theorizing of sound has taken: It will be apparent that the fashionable idealist/nominalist framework sets the agenda. A phenomenology of the film experience reveals that these film sound theories have offered a misleading picture of our experience of sound in cinema. Once the misleading picture has been exposed, it will be possible to intervene in the ongoing dialogue about cinematic sound to offer a phenomenological alternative.

The fantasmatic body

In two articles,[2] Mary Ann Doane exposes a process of repression inherent in what is called "the classic style of filmmaking," or "the dominant mode of filmmaking practice." What she alleges as repressed is the material heterogeneity of the sound film; as she analyzes it, the film work involved in wedding sounds to visuals in a film is effaced so as to maximize an illusion of the real and position a unified subject.[3] On familiar grounds, forcefully enunciated by Baudry,[4] she contends that creation and maintenance of the illusion of the real serves important bourgeois ideological purposes.

The Baudrian argument is that the cinematic apparatus transforms what is before it but conceals that transformation by effacing traces of it. Bourgeois ideology in general functions in much the same way, masking its operations and presenting its object as natural when it is really a product of ideology.[5]

Doane argues that the way sound is utilized in classic cinema contributes to the constitution of a *fantasmatic body*[6] within the film text. Instead of using sound recording and sound editing to emphasize the separateness of visuals and sound in our experience of the film – the true state of affairs in our experience of film (as, for instance, Godard does in *Sympathy for the Devil*) – the classic cinema hides what is in fact the case, namely, that there are just sounds in our experience and there are just visuals in our experience with no real connections existing between them.[7] What the classic cinema does is to make it *seem* as if the sounds and visuals belong to a body; this body has the visual qualities we see and emits the sounds we hear. Spectators of the film are addressed by the film with a particular point of identification, the fantasmatic body, serving to anchor the experience. This body authorizes and sustains certain relationships between sound and image, and has several important characteristics:

The body reconstituted by the technology and practices of the cinema … offers a support as well as point of identification for the subject addressed by the film. The attributes of this fantasmatic body are first and foremost unity and presence-to-itself.[8]

Unity is thus a crucial characteristic arising from the film practice for Doane. It seems to spectators that there is unity when in fact there are just images and sounds. The dialogue we hear belongs to the fantasmatic body (thus, according to Doane, confirming speech as an individual property right, with obvious ideological consequences).[9] She points out that the use of sound carries with it the potential risk of exposing the film work; the dominant cinema is mindful of this risk but aims to surmount it.[10]

In this act of concealing the work of the cinematic apparatus, a fostering of a misrecognition occurs. Instead of the film exploring its potential to reveal the dissociation of image or representation from object, or sign from referent, or signifier from signified, the classic use of sound makes it seem that we see human individuals (fictional though they may be) who have visual appearances, speak and emit sounds, none of which we are actually experiencing. The cinematic apparatus promotes the impression that the senses of the fantasmatic body cannot be split.

Doane thinks it fruitful to analyze the relationship between visuals and sounds in terms of three concepts of space through which the unities of sounds and visuals are achieved:

1. *diegetic* space, the space constructed by the film;
2. the *visible* space of the screen, which contains the visual signifiers; and
3. the *acoustical* space of the movie theater in which sounds are present in a way that visuals are not.[11]

These spaces exist simultaneously for the spectator, but the diegetic space may be acknowledged also by characters in the film. The classic narrative film works to deny the existence of the last two spaces while making credible the first. Doane proposes that Lacan's notion of the invocatory drive, the spectators desire to hear, explains the appeal of the voice in cinema, that is, spectators thrive on being unheard as well as unseen in their voyeurism and eavesdropping activity.

Aural objects

Another influential writing on film sound, that of Christian Metz, posits a fundamental difference between the visual and the aural in film experience.[12] In marking this difference, he relies upon a distinction with a long history in the field of philosophy – the distinction between primary and secondary qualities. As Metz states the distinction:

The primary qualities ... determine the list of objects (substances) and the secondary qualities ... correspond to attributes applicable to these objects.[13]

He explains that "the primary qualities are in general the visual and tactile while the secondary qualities are auditory and olfactory (an aroma is not an object) and certain visual qualities such as color." It is one of Metz's contentions, using the primary–secondary quality distinction that sound can never be off-screen in cinema.[14] His argument is that either a sound is audible or it isn't; when the sound exists, it cannot possibly be situated or not situated within the interior of the screen rectangle. This is so because it is the nature of sounds to diffuse themselves throughout the entire space surrounding spectators.

By contrast, when a visual element is situated off-screen, it really is outside of the screen space: We do not see it, but can infer its off-screen location from what we have seen and are seeing. However, in the case of a sound, we still hear it, in a sense, when it is off-screen. From this analysis, Metz is led to call for a language to capture adequately the nature of aural objects rather than utilizing terms that are appropriate for "the corresponding substance which is ... the visible object, which has emitted the sound."[15]

Metz contends that "the perceptual object is a constructed unity, socially constructed and also a linguistic entity."[16] As such, Metz points out that the distinction between subject here and object out there that we perceive visually and/or aurally is put aside. In this way, as he notes, his semiological analysis is quite removed from that of a phenomenological alternative, where the subject perceives an independently existing object.[17]

From his analysis, Metz elicits a difference between visual qualities and aural qualities. Auditory qualities optimally undergo no appreciable loss in relation to the corresponding sound in the real world, whereas visuals do.[18]

A phenomenological analysis of cinematic sound

These analyses of cinematic sound have the characteristic idealist/nominalist cast to them. Spectators experience only visuals and sounds when they perceive representations. The problem they set for themselves is to assume this picture of cinematic experience, then account for spectators' apprehension of individuals being portrayed in cinema exhibiting unities of visuals and sounds that they believe not to be present. Husserlian horizon analysis will serve to counter the false picture of the experience of sounds in cinema.

When we perceive an object, within film experience or outside of it, we ascribe more to it than we experience in the moment. When we look at a tree from in front, we see the front side of it but perceive a tree with a back side. We perceive that this tree has been in this place in the moments before our perceptual act, that it has roots through which it gains nourishment, and many other things that we do not now see. In the language of phenomenology, perceivers "intend" the object of their perception.

When we experience a sequence in a sound film, we do not see visuals and hear sounds separately and then connect them to the body to which they belong – a fantasmatic body – which is the anchor for our experience. Hitchcock's *The Birds* will serve as an illustration. When we experience the film, the audience intends individuals, Melanie Daniels and Mitch Brenner: They are intended as present in the fictional space; they are intended as speaking to one another. We do not see and hear all of these whole fictional individuals in any moment of our experience of the film, just as in everyday life we do not see and hear all of any real individuals in any moment. Nevertheless, we intend whole individuals in both real-life and fictional situations, that is, individuals with characteristic looks, manner of speaking, desires, intentions, histories, and so forth.

A genetic fallacy is involved in making the film experience different from the everyday life experience. That the visuals and sounds we per-

fallacy!

ceive in a film may have been collected separately in the shooting phase of the filmmaking process and are now played together in the movie theater (as we experience the film) has nothing to do with what we perceive in experiencing the film. In perceiving the characters in the film in the screening, we intend a whole individual, for example, Melanie Daniels in *The Birds*. She is a fictional person, to be sure, but a whole individual whose visual appearance, speech, and movements we perceive, whose desires and intentions we do not now see and hear but intend.

With this phenomenological notion of intending and horizons guiding recognition of the role of visuals and sounds in our perception of film characters, there is no need to posit as Doane does, a fantasmatic body as the locus of the uniting of visuals and sounds, a body that authorizes and sustains illusory connections. We really perceive the fictional character Melanie Daniels; it is not an illusion that we do so. The concept of a fantasmatic body is an unnecessary hypothesization.*

With respect to Christian Metz's claim that sound cannot be off-screen whereas visuals can be, it need only be pointed out that he is either marking a tautology and therefore offering an unuseful analysis or he is providing a false picture of film sound experience. As Melanie Daniels rows a boat across Bodega Bay toward the Brenner home in *The Birds,* there is a shot wherein the sound of the waves lapping against the boat is heard. Spectators properly perceive the sounds as waves lapping around Melanie's boat, and that Melanie is still out in the boat on the way to the Brenners' even though what we see is only a long shot of the Brenner home from a distance.

Appreciators of the film intend the off-screen sound as belonging to the body of water surrounding Melanie's boat just as they intend Melanie as still in the boat on the way to the Brenner home. The sounds (the waves lapping at the boat) and the visuals (Melanie in the boat) are off-screen but suggested by what we have seen and heard together with what we now see and hear. It is not an essentially different case than seeing a tree from the front and intending a tree with a front, a back, and a history of standing in this spot.

Metz wants the visual to be complete in itself in some important way. It is both a substance as well as an attribute; we are supposed to have a presentation of a substance, Melanie, and her visual appearance – just so tall, just so slim, with such and such color hair, with such and such a quality of voice, and so forth. We are also supposed to have only an attribute in the case of the sound – lapping of waves;

---

* In a similar vein, Bill Rothman[19] has argued persuasively that the concept of suture, with its hypotheses of a ghost or other, is an unnecessary framework for explaining such sequences from *The Birds.*

this sound has attributes such as pitch, intensity, duration, and so forth, but there is no substance, according to Metz. Such an analysis is not justified by anything in our experience. A wave is as much a substance as Melanie or the boat. Moreover, it is not fruitful for Metz to adopt his other argument in attempting to make his claim about the non–off-screen status of sounds. It is true by definition – it is tautologically true – that sounds cannot be either on-screen or off-screen in the way visuals can be. Within the rectangular screen space, only visuals may be present. No sounds can be in a visual surface space by definition. Nothing of importance follows about what capacities the film has via its sound to induce áudiences to imagine what objects exist out of sight of the camera in the world of the film. The visuals in the screen space and the sounds we hear guide our perception to an independently existing entity, Melanie Daniels, a fictional character. Melanie is not in the screen but what we see on the screen guides our intending of Melanie.

The primary–secondary quality distinction has been a notoriously difficult one to develop in perception theory. It only seems to get in the way for Metz's analysis of cinematic sound. Needed are concepts from the theory of perception such as Husserl's notion of horizon and intentionality, which capture the dynamics we find in our experience of cinema.

The female voice

Feminist film theory has followed the pattern of contemporary film theory in looking for concepts that may be assimilated to the idealist/ nominalist framework. In "Dis-Embodying the Female Voice,"[20] Kaja Silverman theorizes cinematic sound in a context in which visuals and sounds are separate elements within our experience of a film that must be joined together. She takes as her starting point the familiar view that the female is the object of the gaze in dominant cinema, "excluded from authoritative vision not only at the level of the enunciation but at that of the fiction."[21]

Silverman further argues that "the female subject as she has been constructed by Hollywood cinema is denied any active role in discourse" and "emerges only within discourse. . . . [O]nce inside the symbolic order she has no more access to her biological real than does her masculine counterpart."[22]

Silverman remarks on discursive authority as follows:

The female subject . . . is excluded from positions of discursive authority both inside and outside the diegesis: she is confined not only to safe places within the story . . . but to the safe place *of* the story.[23]

She then connects this analysis of the female subject with cinematic sound theory: "synchronization provides the means of that confinement."[24] Silverman proceeds to provide a conceptual map of sound–image relationships in film experience. She contends that there is a rule of synchronization. This rule involves referring to the alignment of the human form with the human voice. There obtains correlatively

the representation of a homogeneous thinking subject whose exteriority is congruent with its interiority. The marriage of sound and image is thus performed ... under Cartesian auspices.[25]

This Silvermanian analysis entails that the body be read through the voice and the voice through the body, a practice that "drastically curtails the capacity of each for introducing into the narrative something heterogeneous or disruptive."[26] She explains that such homogeneity in practice may be expressed as "it minimizes the number and kinds of connotations which can be activated."[27]

Silverman is regarding narrative as a way of organizing the visuals we see and the sounds we hear as we experience a film. Narrative is but one of many possible ways in which such sensations may be organized. At least two possible ways of organizing these visuals and sounds present themselves: The visual and the auditory sensations may be synchronized so that they denote something or they may be organized so as to foster connotations that can disrupt any audience's sense of narrative and of the union of visuals and sounds.

The nominalist undergrowth of Silverman's conceptualization should be apparent. Visual sensations and auditory sensations are individual things taken as joined together in experience of the classic cinema but are not really joined. Spectators of classic cinema are manipulated to organize according to narrative codes. Spectatorship is describable as acts of reading – for example, reading body through the voice and vice versa.

With a phenomenological conceptualization in mind, Silverman's account may be seen to diverge from the actual experience *of* cinema. Where Silverman posits perception of visual and auditory sensations, phenomenology has apperception of hyletic data. Where Silverman has mediation of visual and auditory sensations via any number of possible codes, phenomenology has experience of events occurring, the perception of which is mediated by apperception of hyletic data and noemata.

Let's again take the boat sequence from *The Birds* to illustrate the differences in theoretical approach. A phenomenological analysis gives a picture of the audience experiencing events: Melanie gets on the boat, rides out into Bodega Bay, moves toward the Brenner home,

codetermine ~~pro~~ noemata

arrives at the landing. Sometimes during the boat ride, the audience sees Melanie rowing; other times, the audience does not see her but rather has a view of the distant Brenner home from out in the bay. Mediating spectatorial grasp of these events are apperception of hyletic data – awarenesses of visuals and sounds, for example, we see the boat fill a certain amount of the frame in one shot; we hear the sounds of the waves lapping but see no boat in another. We have heard Melanie speak to Mitch Brenner and others in Bodega Bay; we see her negotiate the use of the boat with the handler. The audience codetermines the noemata, the awareness of which mediates the experience of these events.

The audience does *not join* these visuals with these sounds in order to construct events, for example, Melanie rowing the boat to the Brenner home. The audience codetermines the noemata that mediate the recognition of the overall event – rowing the boat to the Brenner home and the smaller events associated with it, for example, advancing through the waters of the bay, sighting the Brenner home, moving ever closer to the landing, and so forth. Audience perception is constrained via relevant horizons to perceive these events.

In the sequences where Melanie and others in the town are attacked by the birds, it would be Silverman's view that when Melanie speaks, we see certain things and hear certain sounds and dialogue, but we do not hear the character Melanie speaking as we see her. Everything about our experience of those sequences ensures that we do perceive the character Melanie speaking as we see her. Moreover, this phenomenological analysis of sound in a film such as *The Birds* would apply not only to the external appearances of things but also to the representations of inner states. The intentions, desires, feelings, and/or repressions we ascribe to Melanie Daniels in *The Birds* as a whole and in the bird attack sequences and in the boat sequence are not constructed out of separate visuals and separate sounds but rather are perceived as characteristics of the independently existing fictional person, Melanie Daniels.

With a proper understanding of the role of sound in cinematic experience, some of Silverman's observations about the female subject in film may be questioned. In the sequences where birds attack the townspeople and Melanie Daniels, the look of her body and the sound of her voice are *not* portrayed either with or without synchronicity of visuals and sounds, though with respect to visual and sound hyletic data there is synchronicity. The intended individual Melanie Daniels is neither inside nor outside of a symbolic order within the film as a whole or its bird attack sequences or its boat sequence. She may be portrayed in conformity with her biological reality or not, depending on the nature of the portrayal. That the visual and auditory hyletic data have as a feature synchronicity only contributes to the codetermination of the mediating noemata. Melanie, like real women outside of the Hitchcock film, exists independently of any discourse. The cinematic discourse used to portray Melanie and, for example, the English language used to describe women in everyday life outside the movies, extends only to the noemata. Neither discourse extends to fictional individuals such as Melanie nor to real individuals, say, Allan Casebier. Both Melanie and Allan can or cannot have access to their biological reality, depending on how they proceed to know. There is nothing about discursive context per se that determines success or failure.

As to the reference in Silverman to a Cartesian self-conception, Silverman, like so many contemporary theorists, is drawing a distinction without a difference. The manner in which Descartes attempted to resolve the mind–body problem has been regarded as unsatisfactory to an enormously varied number of positions from the seventeenth century to the present, for example, for Hume, for Kant, for Husserl. One need not agree with a Cartesian analysis of the self to hold a view that there is a unified self experiencing the world and films and characters in films. Indeed, there are at least two rival general conceptual frameworks for accounting for the nature of the self. One posits a unified self, the other posits a many-selves conception. Both frameworks can account for all human behavior. That either one is comprehensive in explanation cannot be a reason for preferring it over the other. The one-self conception proposes that the self lasts through time, exists independently of the experiences it has, and its lasting through time is not determined by the objects it experiences or its acts of consciousness. The many-selves conception, so popular in contemporary film theory, proposes that each situation determines the nature of identity and that there are only individuals in each circumstance that acquire *senses* of self that are illusory. We may be in a post-Cartesian era in that contemporary film theory disagrees with Descartes's view about the self, but, if so, we have been in it for such a long time and through so many alternative accounts of the self that to make the observation about having gone beyond Descartes seems unnecessary to mention and fails to take into account a most viable alternative account to that of contemporary film theory: namely, that there is a self that perceives the film, that codetermines the noemata, and that responds to the dispositional properties of the film to affect the audience.

The fabula

Another of the unnecessary entities of contemporary film theory is the fabula. Its appearance in the theory of film criticism occurs in David Bordwell's development of a theory of norms, intrinsic and extrinsic in nature, that govern cinematic representations. In his *Ozu and the Poetics of Cinema,*[1] Bordwell applies a theory of norms first developed in his earlier works.[2] His writing on the Ozu canon is always illuminating, providing an important corrective to prior critical interpretations. The theory of norms, however, is deeply set into the idealist/nominalist cast, which unnecessarily limits the effectiveness of those aspects of the work addressing cinematic representations in Ozu.

Bordwell provides us with a phenomenoloy of the experience of a film as prelude to introducing the theory of norms:

A film begins. Quickly or slowly the audience starts to understand it [the film], the story it "tells," the way it represents space and time, what is likely to come next. The film ends. The spectator has understood – perhaps not everything, but something. (*OPC*, 73)

Bordwell then gives an account of the process involved in comprehending the narrative, drawing upon his theory of norms. His project is the development of a historical poetics of cinema with application to the Ozu film work. The term 'poetics,' he tells us, is derived from *poiesis,* or active-making. This characterization of the meaning of *poiesis* for the Greeks does not capture what they meant. Though there is a relationship to the Greek verb "to make," in the use of *poiesis*, a poetics was related to making only insofar as it was a subcategory of *producing things:* For the characterization of poetics as active-making there should be substituted a notion of poetics as providing a conceptual map of an art experience, as it was for Aristotle,* with no bias built in about the nature of that experience, that is, whether it involves an active versus passive relationship with the art object, whether the experiencer makes anything, and so forth. *Poiesis* was used in this context to refer to the making of art, whatever that turns out to involve.

Bordwell, in another place, describes how 'poetics' "refers to the study of how films are put together and how, in determinate contexts, they elicit particular effects" (*OPC*, 1), which is a more fruitful characterization that should have been used in providing the phenomenology of film experience. It is, however, the notion of the active-maker, the constructor of the story, that is attractive for Bordwell. In describing the relationship of the viewer to the film and its story, he tells us:

The viewer... needs skills of narrative comprehension for in fact the film does not tell the story; it prompts the spectator to *construct* the story on the basis of

---

* Aristotle says, in *De Poetica:* "Our subject being poetry, I propose to speak not only of the art in general but also of its species and their respective capacities; of the structure of plot required for a good poem; of the number and nature of the constituent parts of a poem."[3]

the syuzhet, the style, and many other schemata which the spectator has acquired.

...

The viewer...needs at least some knowledge of extrinsic norms of film narration – those bodies of conventions, developed across the history of cinema,
that mobilize syuzhet and style into patterns that guide spectators in understanding the stories they help make. (*OPC*, 73)

The idealist underpinnings are palpable in this account of narration.
The spectator constructs the story: The story is something that spectators "help make."

In his theory of narration, the *syuzhet* is an essential element. It is
the substance and sequence of narrative events presented in the film
(*OPC*, 51). Bordwell gives an example of *syuzhet* from Ozu's *Tokyo
Story* (*Toyko monogatari*).

Tokyo Story begins with the elderly father and mother packing to visit their
children in the city; in the next scene, the couple arrive in their son's Tokyo
household. These scenes constitute distinct syuzhet components. (*OPC*, 51)

Another essential element of filmic representation for Bordwell is
the *fabula*, "the total system of story events, explicit or implicit,"
which is a construction of the spectator; as Bordwell puts it, "the syuzhet prompts the spectator to build the fabula" (*OPC*, 51). In the *Tokyo
Story* example, Bordwell offers the conceptual picture that the spectator

must not only construct the narrative units of packing for the trip and arriving
at the son's home; the spectator must also infer the trip itself, which is not
dramatized in the syuzhet. (*OPC*, 51)

The fabula in *Tokyo Story*, which the audience constructs out of the
syuzhet, would include "the action complex of leaving home/travel/
visit to son/travel/arriving in Tokyo" (*OPC*, 51). Bordwell's idea is that,
since we perceive only part of the trip, we must infer the trip. The *syuzhet* is apparently given in spectators' experience: The fabula is constructed by the spectators out of *syuzhet*.

While it is true that there is a rather large ellipsis in *Tokyo Story*, it
has no bearing on the nature of what is called *syuzhet* and fabula
here. The trip is, of course, simply nothing more than packing, riding
on the train, visit to son, more travel, arriving. If the Ozu film were to
show all elements in the travel complex except one – say, it excluded
the stop off to visit a son – the Bordwellian view would entail that we
still do not see the trip but only *syuzhet* events from which the trip is
inferred as a construction. The ellipses do not make spectator perception into a constructive activity; inference may be involved but it is in-

volved on discovery models as well. Fabula is no more a constructed entity than *syuzhet*. With horizon analysis in mind, it is a correct account of our experience of the trip sequence in *Tokyo Story* to say that from the very beginning, we are experiencing the trip. We can imagine story developments that would cancel the sequence portraying a trip to Tokyo, for example, the characters turn out to be actors pretending to take a trip in order to fool the audience. Even though we never see all of the trip – and we do not see all of such a trip in any film – even though there are gaps and ellipses, and unseen aspects, the ellipses in the *syuzhet* do not call for spectator activity of filling-in in order to construct the fabula.

Bordwell addresses the gaps in the *syuzhet* in the following passage:

As the [*Tokyo Story*] example suggests, the syuzhet invariably contains some gaps in presenting the fabula, and the choice and control of these gaps contribute mightily to the overall effect of the film . . . I shall employ the term "diegesis" to refer to the total world of the fabula – its spatio-temporal frame of reference, its furnishings, and the characters that dwell and act within it. (*OPC*, 51–2)

Thus, the fabula is the story that takes place in the diegesis built upon the narrative events explicitly presented in the *syuzhet*.

Phenomenology offers a much different picture, much more in touch with the experience of film narrative. We do not perceive events the way the concept of the *syuzhet* would lead us to think. Instead, we pass through such events (apperceive them) in a way that mediates our apprehension of the trip as the overall event depicted and composed of the smaller explicitly given events. Events in narratives, of course, appear with ellipses that would not ordinarily be found in many everyday life events, but in no way does the presence of ellipses warrant an assumption that spectators construct the events in the narrative.

In delineating the process whereby *syuzhet* prompts spectator construction of the fabula, Bordwell explains the role of extrinsic and intrinsic norms. These norms are constitutive of the fabula constructed. Bordwell describes spectator activity in forming the fabula:

The theory emphasizes the activity of the spectator. . . . The viewer is constantly holding assumptions, building and testing hypotheses, drawing inferences, and arriving at conclusions. The spectator seeks to distinguish pertinent events . . . posit causal and temporal connections among them, and unify the material the syuzhet presents . . . since a film, like a novel or play, unfolds in time, the spectator's construction is subject to constant revision and recasting. A poetics of cinema must recognize that narrative films are so made as to exploit the time-bound nature of viewing. (*OPC*, 52)

This account makes narrative a product of *inductive* activity, an inferential process in which explicitly given events are fashioned into story on the bases of hypotheses. In experiencing a film, no such process is occurring. Spectators are intuitively apprehending the narrative, including events, objects, persons, states of affairs. Hypotheses are not used; we do not proceed via inductive inferences from smaller parts to form a larger entity – the fabula. Rather, as discussed, perceivers apprehend an independently existing narrative, a process involving intuition, fulfillment, horizon, noema, noesis, hyle, and so forth. In comprehending narrative experienced at a screening in *Tokyo Story*, spectators' apprehension of the trip arises together with our apprehension of what Bordwell regards as *syuzhet* events – packing, riding, arriving – with the latter apperceived while the former is perceived.

Bordwell describes extrinsic norms as guiding spectator construction of the fabula and stylistic patterning. He posits these norms as neither "in the text" nor "in the viewer." He proposes that the norms are not in the text because "they precede, as hypotheses, apprehension of the film," hence they could not be in the text, which arises out of the interaction of (1) spectator and (2) what the experience of the film prompts us to perceive. He proposes that the norms are not in the viewer because they are intersubjectively valid. By means of the norms, Bordwell regards the viewer as giving a reading of the film.[4]

An idealist framework such as that on which Bordwell is relying leads to difficulties in identifying the locus of concepts such as norms. If norms are neither in the viewer nor in the text, then one wonders what locus they have? Bordwell has sound reasons for neither objectifying them nor making them subjective. The realist model can accommodate Bordwell's insights about norms without leaving their status problematic as he does.

The extrinsic and intrinsic norms are horizons that guide our intuitive grasp of an independently existing narrative. They are not *in* the *syuzhet* events; they are not *in* the fabula; they are not merely our own subjective way of looking at things but rather it is our disposition to utilize the norms as horizons in codetermining the noemata. The ways in which the *Tokyo Story* trip appears to us are the noemata; they mediate our grasp of the trip as part of the film's narrative, a narrative that has come into existence because of the creative activities of the filmmakers and that exists out of our reach to constitute *Tokyo Story*.

Bordwell describes the extrinsic norms relevant for comprehending an Ozu film such as *Tokyo Story* as, respectively, classical norm, art-cinema norm, and parametric norm (*OPC*, 176–7). Intrinsic norms arise within the film experience itself in a way that extrinsic norms do not. Bordwell describes the norms as follows:

Intrinsic norm; Especially important is the tendency of the film to establish, in its early portions, an intrinsic norm of narrational method that serves as a stable base for spectatorial assumptions and hypotheses. Of course, if later stretches of the syuzhet do not adhere to this norm, the viewer will be confronted with the need to revise the initial schema. A film might begin by restricting us to what one character knows and then abruptly widen our knowledge in a fashion that asks us to discard certain inferences about that character's actions. (*OPC*, 52)

The most influential of the extrinsic norms is the classical, which

encourages the spectator to build the film around a strong cause-effect chain proceeding from clear-cut psychology and working itself out to a definite resolution. The narration is assumed to be reliable, at least most of the time and in most genres. (*OPC*, 176)

The art-cinema norm encourages the viewer to build the film around psychologically ambiguous characters and a notion of an elusive external reality. The viewer is also expected to be alert for an overt and unreliable narration that evokes a range of tentatively applicable connotations. The film is assumed to be a vehicle for the director's vision of life, conveyed chiefly through symbolic actions and objects (*OPC*, 177). The parametric norm takes "the patterning of film style as being at least intermittently as important as narrative systems. The spectator is to attend to how the film establishes an intrinsic stylistic norm and then varies that through additive and variational processes" (*OPC*, 177).

These norms are indeed at work in the experience of the Ozu films, but the idealist form to their description is unnecessary and misleading. They may be refashioned in terms of the realist framework, preserving all of Bordwell's insight while avoiding the problems that their idealist cast brings about. They are horizons that guide our intuitive processes. In experiencing *Tokyo Story*, we intend a trip with all of its constituent parts. In guiding our intuitions, the critic may mention the presence of these norms by helping us to perceive what he or she has perceived, the trip from home to Tokyo. The norms are not systematic codes but useful ways of eliciting the proper direction for intuition and fulfillment to obtain. They function only in a context where intentionality is occurring; where spectators are intending objects, events, and persons. They are not concerned with forming and testing hypotheses about whether a trip is being taken but rather with orienting intuition to fulfillment of an intending that occurred from the beginning of the fictional action. Bordwell makes plausible that these orienting forms may guide the wider process of recognizing what and how the film depicts.

The diegesis

The diegesis is the total world of the fabula – its spatio-temporal frame of reference, its furnishings, and the characters that dwell and act within it.

– David Bordwell[1]

As we have seen, Bordwell, like so many contemporary film theorists, feels the need to posit diegesis, another of those entities ubiquitous in idealist/nominalist film theorizing. Instead of the realist model of spectators perceiving independently existing fictional events in a fictional space–time, we are told that there is a diegetic world in which fabula takes place, with both fabula and diegesis imagined by the spectator. Postulating a diegesis is a necessary step in idealist/nominalist accounts of representation since the spectator is not perceiving a space or events like a trip to Tokyo or objects like the "furnishings" that Bordwell speaks of but is rather constructing these entities.

Noel Burch also utilizes a concept of a diegesis in his theory about the Japanese cinema (see earlier discussion). He tells us that the diegesis is the imaginary referent or sum of referents of a film: Most simply, he says:

The diegesis is for instance the world of Balzac which his readers enter, those imagined drawing rooms and cobbled streets, those imagined people, their characters, their souls.[2]

Burch assumes that assigning this meaning to 'diegesis' entails that diegesis and narrative are in no sense equivalent "since there is so much more to diegesis than narrative."[3] What he seems to mean is that a description of narrative would tell you what happened in the film while a description of diegesis would get at the fictional environment in the world of the work. If you knew just the narrative, you would know what happened, but you would know neither what the world of the work looked like nor felt like nor how it affected the spectator.

Clarity is needed about the nature of this crucial term – diegesis – in the contemporary film critics' language in order to assess its value in analyzing narration.

One of the first things you notice about diegesis is that not everyone uses it to mean the same thing. The term was introduced into film theory by Etienne Souriau to mean the sum of a film's denotations.[4] Christian Metz explains that diegesis means

> the narration itself, but also the fictional space and time dimensions implied in and by the narrative, and consequently the characters, the landscapes, the events, and other narrative elements, in so far as they are considered in their denoted aspect.[5]

Bill Nichols claims that use of the term 'diegesis' in criticism allows us "to designate the imaginary world of the fiction."[6] Additionally, such designation of the imaginary world of the fiction is accomplished without building in a bias toward realism or even illusionism, as for example, the term 'mimesis' does. Nichols proposes that use of the term as so formulated, "guards against the danger of short-circuit leaps between reality and realism."[7] In order to avoid what he takes to be an error in supposing that a documentary can somehow capture or project reality, Nichols formulates a distinction between diegesis and 'diegesis,' where the former designates the spatiotemporal continuity comparable to that in fiction while the latter refers to the imaginary rhetorical ordering of events within the work. Seeing 'diegesis' with quotes around it will remind us that denotation does not constitute capturing or projecting reality.[8]

Burch derives an initial plausibility from a seemingly descriptive character of the concept diegesis. However, if 'diegesis' is to be a descriptive term, standing for the imaginary characters, imaginary drawing rooms, and so forth, it cannot also be possible for, for example, Oshima's cinematic strategies in a film like *Boy* (*Shonen*) to "rupture" the diegesis. The kind of strategies that a Japanese new-wave director such as Oshima utilizes cannot rupture the imaginary space, time, objects, and events of the world of the film. If there are both narrative and diegesis, there always being more to the latter than to the former, diegesis is always there in some form or other. Nothing can rupture or suspend it.

What Burch may have in mind is our absorption in the diegesis, in this imaginary world of objects, events, persons – that is, in a psychic relation to something that is always there in our film experience. In the following quote, he distinguishes between diegesis and diegetic process:

> The diegesis must not ... be treated as a fixed, simple object. ... For the constitution of the diegesis is a process, and a more proper term would indeed be *diegetic process*. It combines a mental process (the development of the spectator's absorption) and a process of writing the implementation on the screen of the codes which catalyse that absorption. The resultant is a diegetic effect, whereby spectators experience the diegetic world as environment. (*TDO*, 19)

If we need to think of there being an entity called 'the diegesis,' which spectators can become absorbed in or not, room can be made for rupturing the absorption by an Oshima film using an array of Brechtian discourses. The question remains, however, is it fruitful to conceptualize film experience in terms of a distinction between narrative and diegesis?

It is clear that the concept of the diegesis flows from the idealist assumption that how the world of the work is and how we know it depends on the activities of the knowing mind. Spectators construct an imaginary world of objects, events, and persons from the materials of their film experience – sensa or *syuzhet* – to create a narrative and a diegesis. Off-screen narration and background music, which characters can hear, are part of the diegesis. Moreover, objects present in the environment of and events occurring to characters are part of the diegesis as well.

What Bordwell conceptualizes as the classical norm governing spectator construction of the fabula – clear-cut psychology, framework of cause-and-effect relationships, movement toward a resolution, a narration that one can trust – do seem to cultivate spectator absorption in events, objects, and characters. By contrast, what Bordwell characterizes as art-cinema norm and especially parametric norm tends to foster heightened awareness of the medium and less absorption in events, objects, and characters, all other things being equal.

Faced with the differing meanings and uses of diegesis, Edward Branigan argues for a restriction of discourse about diegesis to reference to "a diegetic level of narration as opposed to a diegetic object or percept available to a character."[9] In this sense, 'diegesis' refers to an implicit process of evaluation by the spectator of evidence furnished by the text that "bears on the relationship of a character to a world of his or her sensory data."[10] In other proposals for the meaning of 'diegesis' (those of Metz, Nichols, and Burch), Branigan finds a "tendency to fuse narration and narrative together ... which results in applying the concept of diegesis indiscriminately."[11] Branigan argues that speaking of

"diegetic effect" or "diegetic impression" merely perpetuates the confusion without distinguishing whether one is analyzing the methods underlying a judgment or the consequences of the judgment itself. Nor is it of any aid to introduce the terms "denotation" or "connotation," as do Metz and Etienne Souriau, because these terms apply to both narration and narrative.[12]

Branigan further points out that Burch's unfortunate manner of describing diegesis as an "imaginary referent" raises more problems than it solves, since a referent is something located "*outside* of the symbolic field which points to it."[13]

The realist framework developed here provides justification for going one step further than Branigan suggests. Instead of avoiding some uses of 'diegesis' while using others, better to eliminate any reference to diegesis in film criticism. With spectators apprehending independently existing fictional events taking place in fictional spaces utilizing horizons to apprehend them, there is no need to draw the distinctions involved in positing a diegesis. Voice-over narration guides spectator apprehension: Background music keys response. Dialogue and music that characters can hear are part of the fictional situation portrayed. To characterize the situations, characters, events, furnishings, and so forth as imaginary presumes a spectator activity that this phenomenological exploration has shown to be unjustified.

Moreover, the kind of critical assessment of films that the concept of the diegesis is supposed to facilitate may be done without it. For example, the Japanese new wave may be understood without recourse to a conceptualization involving diegesis. Though it is a radical cinema practice, there is nothing about its thematic and stylistic concerns or strategies that requires an analysis of its films in terms of the concept of the diegesis.

The Japanese nouvelle vague developed various cinematic strategies intended to position the spectator more felicitously than had certain well-established practices in film industries in Hollywood, Europe, and even in Japan. One thinks of Yoshida's radically decentered compositions in *Eros Plus Massacre* (*Eros purass gyakusatsu*) or *Confessions among Actresses* (*Kokuhakateki-joy u-ran*); Oshima's dislocational strategies in *Boy* or *Ceremony* (*Gishiki*); Imamura's blurring of traditional distinctions among cinematic genres, styles, and realities in *A Man Vanishes* (*Ningen johatsu*) or *Profound Desire of the Gods* (*Kamigami no fukaki yokuba*), Shinoda's strategies for audience positioning in *Double Suicide* or *Assassination* (*An satsu*).

All of these strategies, styles, and techniques are intended to significantly alter the spectator's relation with not only the film at hand but with cinema as a societal institution in which the spectator seeks experience through film. The analogy between new-wave filmmakers in Japan with counterparts in the French New Wave is apt. Both movements arose at the same time with the former inspired by and derivative from the latter. Both movements sought to decenter spectators, dislocating them in relation to space, time, and action. Oshima's manifesto of the early 1960s has its place in the rise of the Japanese nouvelle vague in that he proposes a counter to a perceived-to-be-dominant cinema. As Burch notes, Oshima called for an overthrow of a basic postulate of traditional cinema, "which since the beginning of sound has held that the picture exists to tell the story" (*TDO*, 327).

The strategies adopted by Oshima and his compatriots of the new wave served to undermine the impression spectators had often had at the cinema, via centered compositions, eyeline match cut-editing, seamless editing, in general, that he or she is an *invisible relay* (*TDO*, 65). Though a conversation could in theory be represented in a variety of ways, including highly abstract ways, highly dislocating ways, and so forth, the fact that such careful attention has been given to make the lines of perspective in screen space converge for spectators and to produce eyeline matchings confirms that classic cinema provides spectators with a spectacle made for themselves (as product to be consumed).

In the Japanese new wave, spectators are confronted with perceptual surfaces/textures that do not give them a sense that what is being experienced exists for the purpose of consumption. In Yoshida's films of the 1960s and 1970s, radically decentered compositions are the principal vehicles for altered and fruitful subject positioning. Sudden shifts to decentering produce a sense of abstractness to what one sees in the long walk beneath the cherry blossoms in *Eros Plus Massacre;* in this sequence the protagonist and one of his women appear only as small heads bobbing on the lower edge of the black-and-white, wide-screen frame. Composition with black areas predominating and with objects of greatest interest squeezed into a corner are the mode of expression in *Confessions among Actresses.* Mixed with this strategy of decentering are radically unrealistic scenes in which crucial events are staged and lyrically elaborated. Allied effects include as Burch puts it, "more directly Brechtian procedures, such as theatricalized interpolations, title boards, mixtures of historical fact and fiction, past and present [in *Eros Plus Massacre*]" (*TDO*, 348).

In the Oshima films, for example, *Boy* discussed earlier decentered compositions are utilized to dislocate the viewer from a consumer relation with the film. An accompanying music track of atonal music further removes the action of the film from the texture of realistic naturalism. Before the *Kanji* for "The End" appears on the screen at the end of *The Ceremony*, the screen goes black offering no image for the audience to relate to; theatrical rendering replaces cinematic style suddenly and perturbingly in Oshima's *Night and Fog in Japan* (*Nihon no yoru to kiri*).

In Imamura's *A Man Vanishes,* a real-life search for a woman's missing husband is led by an actor playing a fictional investigator in the film. This actor leads the real-life wife in search of her real-life missing husband as Imamura's camera tracks their activity. Gradually, there develops a real-life love affair between actor pretending to be investigator and the real-life wife. Their search for the man who vanished culminates in the discovery of the probable murder of the missing man by the wife's sister. In the climactic scene in the film, set seemingly in a fictional teahouse but in actuality (but unbeknownst to the wife and her sister), set on a disguised sound stage, the real-life sisters confront one another about the accusations of murder while continuing to enact the search before the camera. Imamura's blurring of the usual mainstream cinema distinctions between documentary and reality becomes a strategy for positioning the spectator in a productive relationship with the film. At this climactic moment, the walls of the fake teahouse fall, revealing the sound stage with Imamura remarking on the blurring of fiction and reality.

Thus, a concept such as diegesis is unnecessary for an understanding of these cinematic strategies of the Japanese new wave even though conceptually mapping them would be a supposed value of the diegetic concept. Nouvelle vague filmmakers of Japan utilized strategies that may be accounted for better in terms of phenomenology.

When we examine our experience introspectively, we discover two different attitudes we may take toward a film or play. A basic phenomenological distinction is between two types of distance: one psychological and the other emotional. When perceivers have psychic distance,[14] their situation is akin to what Husserl refers to as neutrality modification. Spectators' usual practical and personal concerns with objects, events, and persons are set aside, permitting them to focus on the spectacle before them. The local yokel who climbs onto the stage to come to the assistance of the heroine in her struggles with the villain in the melodrama does not have this distance. Acquisition of psychic distance is an achievement. One either has distance or does not. One cannot realize that William H. Smith's melodrama *The Drunkard* is just a play – and thus have psychic distance – just a little.

By contrast, when one has emotional distance toward an art object, whether film, play, or whatever, it is characteristically possessed to a certain degree or other. A jealous husband and I may attend a performance of *Othello* together. Though he knows full well what he witnesses is just a play – hence he has psychic distance – he may be so consumed by anger and jealousy over his wife's infidelities that he cannot maintain much distance at all; his positioning is quite near emotional immersion. At the same time, I who am not suffering from a similar jealousy and am a historian of the Shakespearean theater, am rather distanced from the play that night, focusing my attention on the historical authenticity of the performance but not feeling any distinctive feelings at all.

With this distinction between psychic and emotional distance in mind, we can say all that we need to say and say it better than if we were to use the concept of the diegesis. For instance, decentered compositions in the Yoshida films position spectators at psychic and emo-

tional distance. They are inhibited from taking an attitude long culti-
vated by classic cinema that what is perceived in the film is spectacle
designed for consumer consumption. The spectators are rather removed correspondingly to a considerable degree of emotional distance
from the Yoshida film. In this state, they primarily contemplate the
characters' actions rather than feel emotions characteristic of identification (e.g., sympathy, empathy, etc.). From this positioning, they can
take a critical stance toward the human situations portrayed rather
than be manipulated by emotions that usually arise as a result of the
experience of the classic cinema.

It is, however, important to realize that it is toward human relationships and human character that the spectators are positioned differently, not toward some posited diegesis. We can fully understand what
Yoshida is trying to do by identifying the relation of spectator to fic-
tionalized human subjects. To attempt to identify the viewers' relationships to the ingredients proposed for the concept of the diegesis has
the difficulties enumerated earlier, and nothing in our experience
really suggests that such relationships take place. Once we have noted
the various psychic and emotional relationships of distance or immersion to the film as constituted by such terms as human characters, human relationships, objects, events, narrative, we gain nothing by
making the additional step of trying to pinpoint spectator positioning
in relation to the fictional space and time, the sum of the film's referents or the imaginary world of the film. We have already identified
those relationships with concepts like psychic and emotional distance.
It is only the attractiveness of finding a concept like that of the diegesis that fits the idealist/nominalist mold that accounts for the cur-
rency of 'diegetic,' 'diegesis,' and 'diegetic process' in the contemporary
critics' language.

The concept of the diegesis has, of course, been used for ideological
analysis of film. Absorption of spectators in the diegesis is supposed
to have the potential to position spectators into passive acceptance of
bourgeois illusionism. As Burch puts it:

The stages of formation and the on-going elaboration of the basic mode of representation in the cinema of the West point to an all but universal tendency
within the dominant cinema ... to maximize and generalize the diegetic effect
and this tendency, in turn, must be understood as entering into a dialectical
relationship with cultural and ideological conditioning. (*TDO,* 19).

Much of the argument of this work has been directed against the
concept of illusionism implicit in this quote. Phenomenology provides
the framework for justifying the view that motion picture representations are independently existing entities, real objects in some cases,

not illusory. The assumption in contemporary theory that independently existing entities are not represented by motion pictures leads to the view that the impression spectators have of apprehending real and/or independently existing entities is illusory. The diegesis is then one of the hypothesized entities of contemporary film theory to account for the illusionism, an illusionism that cannot be justified. The conclusion that is warranted is that the diegesis is an unnecessary conceptual flourish, its hypothesization expressive of an unfruitful picture of cinematic representation.

The Imaginary

The notion of the Imaginary, which Jacques Lacan developed[1] and which Christian Metz uses in formulating his view that cinema is an Imaginary signifier,[2] fulfills the requisites for an idealist/nominalist theory of cinematic representation. The theory of the Imaginary is part and parcel of a view of human identity wherein the human subject is constructed by and in a cultural context rather than being transcendent to it, as in the phenomenological account. The unities that are to be found in cinematic representations (and in other aspects of film experience) are not properties of an independently existing object, the film, but products of an unconscious process. The Imaginary is responsible for generating illusory unities. By contrast, phenomenology explains the unities in cinematic representations in terms of conscious processes; although the existing subject is not conscious of the operations of the noema and noesis while in the acts involved in apprehending features of cinematic representations, neither are they part of the *unconscious*.

The Imaginary is a disposition of the individual to behave in certain ways. Noel Carroll suggests that the Imaginary is something like the imagination in older theories of mind in being a faculty.[3] I refer to it as a disposition to avoid situating the concept in a faculty psychology, which is a somewhat old-fashioned conceptualization. This disposition is not instinctual, not present at birth, but rather is acquired during what Lacan calls "the mirror stage," a period of development for the child beginning in the sixth month and continuing to the eighteenth month. This stage is crucial for the child's acquisition of a *sense* of identity. Acquiring this sense of subjecthood is dependent on acquiring the Imaginary.

In this mirror stage, the child's feelings of fragmentation and dependency become replaced by senses of unity and autonomy (both of which are posited by Lacan as illusory). The mirror experience has the outcome of developing within the individual a disposition, the Imaginary. Once acquired, the Imaginary stays with the individual throughout his or her life. It is a disposition of the individual to take self, persons, objects, events, and states of affairs to be unified and to supply the unity when in fact there are no unities in self or other.

At six months the child is, according to the Lacanian theory, ripe for acquisition of the Imaginary. In the prenatal phase, the child has a sense of plenitude. The intervention of birth – separation from the mother – removes this sense of plenitude. Loss is felt; alienation becomes the child's condition. Lacan accordingly makes a sense of loss central to the postnatal condition. This loss becomes a crucial condition for the constitution of the illusory sense of identity, of human subjecthood.

In the mirror phase, the child has an experience of his or her own image in the mirror, which the child misrecognizes him or herself.* The child's feelings of fragmentation and dependency become replaced by a sense of unity and autonomy, conceiving of him or herself as separate from the other and as a unified whole, capable of autonomy based on this misrecognition. The disposition to so regard self and other as unified is now permanently instilled. Lacan describes the experience as follows:

This jubilant assumption of his specular image by the child at the *infans* stage, still sunk in motor incapacity and nursling dependency, would seem to exhibit in an exemplary situation the symbolic matrix in which the I is precipitated in a primordial form, before it is objectified in the dialectic of identification with the other and before language restores to it, in the universal, its function as subject.[5]

The Imaginary has a unifying function for the child in this mirror stage and later on in the life of the individual whenever the Imaginary is triggered. The sense of unity and autonomy comes from outside and from a representation (e.g., what is experienced in the mirror). In distinguishing ourselves as selves, we do so in response to "the other" via the mediation of the Imaginary. What we are and what we desire is promulgated from the earliest times and continues to be promulgated from the outside. Representations continue to have the power to foster

---

* Rick Altman lucidly describes the mirror stage as follows: "According to Lacan, the infant develops between the ages of six to eighteen months from a state where his own mirror image appears to him as another child, to the point where he recognizes the image as himself. It is at this stage that the infant first fully realizes a notion of selfhood. Up to this moment he has related to himself only as a series of separate parts; now, at a time when his powers of vision far outstrip his capacity for coordinated motor action, the child gains a sense of his own unity with the help of a mirror. The eyes are thus the very source of man's sense of Self. This primary identification at the same time presents a significant problem: the mirror image which the child identifies with himself is in fact not the child itself, but only an image. The life of the Self thus begins under the sign of a misapprehension."[4]

false senses of unity and autonomy insofar as the Imaginary may be activated.

For Lacan, there are three essential orders of the psychoanalytic field: the Imaginary, the Symbolic, and the Real.[6] For Lacan, the Symbolic is another disposition acquired in the early years that stays with us throughout our lives. The Symbolic stage of development is for Lacanian psychoanalysis what the Oedipus complex stage is for Freud. In the Symbolic stage, the child acquires social roles, values, and enters language. The Symbolic, unlike the Imaginary, is responsible for senses of difference, division, and heterogeneity. The Imaginary and the Symbolic, when they come into play, conspire in positioning the subject as a unified, autonomous agent with a cultural situation where the individual uses language. Language is conceptualized by Lacan, as with much contemporary film theory, along lines enunciated by Ferdinand de Saussure. Language is diacritical in nature. Under Saussure's analysis,[7] the meanings of terms in a language is disconnected from reference to objects that exist independently of the language; terms have meaning only by means of interrelationships of difference between signs in the given language system.

At the Symbolic stage, the child becomes not only integrated into a system of language but also integrated into codes of conduct, into social relationships. The law is the name of the system with "the name of the father" at the center. The child coming under the law enters simultaneously the order of language, since the order of language and the order of the law are identical.* In entering the law, the child finds his or her place in a system of names diacritically structured around "the name of the father." The child achieves a high degree of subject construction through becoming a language/culture user.

In appropriating the Lacanian notion of the Imaginary for his theory of cinema, Metz is using the psychoanalytic theory analogically. Metz

---

* Rich Altman describes the relationships between the Imaginary and the Symbolic as follows: "The mirror stage corresponds to the Imaginary order. It is followed by the Oedipal stage, during which the child accedes to the Symbolic order, the order of language and of the Father. In Lacan's scenario, the father is assumed absent during the mirror stage, which is dominated by the mother. Once the child achieves primary identification, however, the father intervenes, separating the child from the mother. This separation constitutes the child's first encounter with the Law-of-the-Father, with which he will later identify. It is at this point that the child gains a symbolizing ability closely related to the acquisition of language. In order to represent the mother when she is absent (or any other absent object), the child must resort to meaningful linguistic oppositions.... Eventually, the child succeeds in naming the cause of the mother's absence, and in so doing names the father. This secondary identification with the Name-of-the-Father... permits the child to rise above his dual relationship with the mother and to enter into the triadic relationship basic to the family. In this way the child finally becomes a subject entirely distinct from his parents, prepared to enter into the world of language and of culture and capable of articulating the difference between Imaginary and Real."[8]

finds that adult experience of cinema bears an analogical relationship to the primordial mirror experience. The source of analogy is a common structure, a play of presence and absence, in both the "stade du miroir" and film experience.

The image that the child apprehends in the mirror is present; the child itself is, however, absent from the mirror. The cinematic representation on the cinematic screen is present to the spectator, for example an image of a person or an object is a mountain, but what it signifies (the person or mountain), is absent, that is, it is not in the screening room. Metz is characterizing what is unique to cinema by contrast with the experience of the theater. In theater, a character or object is represented by something that actually is present to the audience, an actor/actress or a prop. Thus the theatrical signifier differs from the cinematic signifier in not involving a play of presence and absence. The theatrical signifier will not trigger the Imaginary; the cinematic signifier will.

Metz analyzes cinematic representation in terms of the Imaginary signifier's play of presence and absence. Due to the strong connection of the experience of the cinema screen with the primordial mirror, film viewers come to identify with the camera, as well as experience voyeuristic pleasure, which leads them to engage in disavowal and fetishism. With respect to the voyeurism, the film spectator is absent from the actor in a way not possible with the theater actor. The cinema spectator sees from an unseen position with respect to disavowal; the process of both believing and not believing at the same time that females have penises and are castrated is found by Metz to have analogs in cinematic experience. In cinema, we both believe and do not believe that the character Annie Hall is there, in an experience of Woody Allen's film *Annie Hall*. With respect to fetishism, there is again the characteristic analogy. For the fetishist, one object stands for a fantasized absent aspect of a female. Metz draws the cinematic analogy as follows:

The cinema fetishist is the person who is enchanted at what the machine is capable of, at the theatre of shadows as such. For the establishment of his full potency for cinematic enjoyment, he must think at every moment (and above all simultaneously) of the force of presence the film has and of the absence on which this force is constructed.[9]

Metz's appeal to unconscious processes to explain the construction of cinematic representation is quadruply problematic, in comparison to the phenomenological model, in that it rests upon:

1. the quite implausible Saussurean diacritical theory of language;
2. argument by analogy, a procedure always fraught with difficulty;

3. the highly questionable theory of mind set forth by Lacan; and
4. a quite forced analysis of cinematic experience itself.

The diacritical theory of language is unable to explain how language learning and communication are possible. Language beginning and language learning require some fixed relations between some words in a language and their referents, relationships that Saussaure and Lacan deny, but their denials were never made plausible.

How, for example, would anyone learn the meaning of the term 'red' in English (or its equivalents in any other language) if he or she were never exposed to any red things existing independently of language? Moreover, how indeed did color terms come into all living languages if the meaning of one term is to be apprehended simply by being led to other terms in the language? Basic to any viable theory of language is a distinction between what is currently called "the extension" and the "intension" of the term – between the object to which the term refers (e.g., all the chairs in the world) and the criterion (or criteria) used in picking out the object from among all other things (e.g., movable seat for one). To have simply the intension for the term 'chair' and the meanings for 'movable' and 'seat' and 'for' and 'one' but not any independent experience of the things that are chairs would preclude a mastery of the term 'chair.' It is obvious that the whole elaborate machinery of Husserl's theory of language explained here would support the necessity of language having independently existing referents.

With respect to arguments by analogy, it need only be said that the most that can be derived from them are suggestive ideas that have to be established on *some other basis*. It is inherent in analogies that for every point of analogy found – such as Metz analogizing that adult viewers and mirror stage children have reduced motor activity and reliance on sight – there are usually more points of disanalogy that are overlooked in drawing the comparison. For instance, as I experience a film, I hear as much as I see in many cases; I can move around the theater as much as I sit and yet have the same experience of the film as if I sat all the way through.

With respect to Lacanian psychoanalysis as a foundation for the belief in the existence of the Imaginary, Noel Carroll has said it well:

Lacan spends almost no methodological energy laying out in the essay in which he postulates the mirror stage...one is taken aback that so much contemporary theory is based upon so little documentation...if the mirror experience is construed metaphorically, doesn't that undercut the analogy between the mirror and film upon which people like Metz rely?[10]

Carroll points out also the equivocations in the use of the term 'unity' in the claims about the unities that the Imaginary creates. Carroll seems correct that 'unity' is being stretched beyond all utility by the theory of the Imaginary as creating unity in human bodies, in images of human bodies, in coherent novels and films, and in selves. As Carroll puts it:

It would seem to be the vagueness and lack of specificity of the operative concept of unity in this [Lacanian] account that is allowing its proponent to treat things as dissimilar as bodies and sentences as if they were functionally equivalent. But the only connection between them seems to be a verbal one. We call bodies unified in virtue of their continuity within the limits of their contour; coherent utterances are unified in virtue of their meaningfulness.[11]

Carroll also points to an incoherence in the Lacanian concept of the Imaginary:

...If we say that the Imaginary is able to use all these different unities to project subject unities because all these different things have the common property of self-identity, then we have traveled in a circle, since it is the Imaginary that is supposed to explain how things are grasped as self-identifiable entities.[12]

Richard Wollheim, in a searching critique of Lacanian psychoanalysis,[13] points out that when it comes to the elaborate Lacanian account of the infant's entry into symbolism, and the attempt to ground psychosexuality in language, it fails to give a plausible theory. It would go beyond the scope of this study of representation to explore, as does Wollheim so well, all of the implausibilities mentioned. In discussing the name of the father phenomenon, Wollheim argues as follows:

Freud, as we know, thought the appearance of the father in the infant's awareness sets up a three-cornered conflict in its mind in which the actors are father, mother, and infant and the stake is the infant's sexual organ. This is the Oedipus conflict. Lacan also talks of a psychic drama in the infant's mind. He gives it the same structure as Freud does, he gives it the same dramates personae as Freud, and he borrows the Freudean title.[14]

Wollheim then describes the drama:

The Lacanian drama is set into being by the name-of-the-father and it is fought over the phallus. Is this a coincidence, or does it show that whatever may be in doubt about the Lacanian scenario, the name-of-the-father and the Phallus must be given a literal significance primarily, if an extended one derivatively? With this, the attempt to ground psychosexuality in the phenomenon of language collapses.[15]

Throughout his analysis of Lacan, Wollheim points out the ways in which Lacan's theory lacks the explanatory power of Freud's, primarily due to Lacan's denial of any instinctual unconscious and his effort to make language the content of the unconscious. Where for Freud principles of association are condensation and displacement, for Lacan they are metonymy and metaphor. In order to get into the unconscious, according to Lacan, something must first be symbolized. Metaphor and metonymy are intrinsic features of language with the result that for Lacan human personality is formed by the impersonal forces of language. But as Wollheim argues, an adequate account must recognize that it is *users* of language who associate not forms of language. Wollheim also notes that maturation has no place in Lacan's model; for Lacan, explanation of psychological phenomena must *not* proceed by reference to the physical but rather be reduced to a theory of symbol acquisition.[16]

As for Metz's description of the film experience upon which he attempts to liken it to the primordial mirror experience, a phenomenology of the experience, of a motion picture belies the status of an imaginary signifier for cinematic representations. The contrast of film with theater experience in establishing that cinema has the Imaginary is unconvincing. Though it is true that there is no way to go from the space of the movie palace in which we sit to the space that Annie Hall inhabits – for there is no intervening space to cross – the same may be said for the experience of theater. We cannot enter the space in which theatrical performances occur; we can only, by rushing onstage, interrupt the performance. Film and theater are like novels in that their portrayal of fictional events and fictional spaces are alike. We are absent from all fictional spaces, a fact from which nothing follows about an alleged triggering of unconscious processes or our apprehension of cinematic representations.

Additionally, phenomenologically the experience of a mirror and the experience of a motion picture are so different as to render the account of the latter by means of the former unilluminating. In a mirror, we see an image of ourselves; when we look at a motion picture on a movie screen, we do not see ourselves. Also sometimes we identify with the view from the camera, even have a *sense* of the camera being like a person, but we never identify with the camera, as Metz's theory requires. To be sure, critics sometimes use the expression "spectators identify with the camera in such and such a sequence," but they must mean that spectators identify with a view had from the position of the camera or have a sense of the camera being like a person, but we never think of ourselves as a camera.

Metz's claims about voyeurism, fetishism, and disavowal being our condition in film experience involves straining our credibility in the extreme, as Carroll so aptly demonstrates in example after example.[17] For instance, no one simultaneously believes and disbelieves that Diane Keaton or Annie Hall are in the screening room with them; they all always believe that Keaton and Hall are not there. Some viewers may be voyeurs (others may be fetishists), but to claim that all viewers are voyeurs is to rob the term of any significant meaning. If I cannot escape being an unseen observer (and I cannot if by definition all viewers are voyeurs because they are sitting in a chair in the theater, not sitting in a chair *in* the movie being screened), the term *voyeur* has none of the psychological meanings it has in any psychoanalytic theory.

Husserl has told us how to perform the reduction, and once having performed the reduction, one can recognize conscious and nonconscious processes at work in the apprehension of cinematic representations. Given that Metz, drawing upon Lacan, has made no plausible case for the operations of unconscious processes of the sort he describes in a supposed constitution of cinematic representations, there seems no reason to take filmic depictions, portrayals, and/or symbolisms as imaginary signifiers; there is rather every reason to regard them as independently existing objects known via the mediation of a subject transcendent to them and the conscious and nonconscious acts he specifies that are involved in their apprehension. The notion of the Imaginary fits in with the idealist/nominalist framework. The Imaginary is intended to account for the seeming occurrence of unity and other universal characteristics as well as for representations where there really are only sensa. The Imaginary is thus antirealist, both ontologically and epistemologically. No doubt fulfilling this function constitutes an important reason for the popularity the concept of the Imaginary has had in contemporary film theory. It would, however, be better to question the underlying idealist/nominalist foundations than seek and find concepts that fit that foundation, no matter how implausible may be arguments to the effect that they really are operative in our experience.

Feminist theories of cinematic representation

A main project of a feminist film theory is no doubt shared by all within the field of cinema studies: Identify those conditions within the motion picture medium that have fostered and continue to maintain an unjust position for women in society. The development of a viable theory of cinematic representation that will further this endeavor of identification has been and will continue to be a priority within the field. The discussion in this section urges the perspective that:

1. feminist film theory has become ensnared in the idealist/nominalist framework and
2. replacement of the perturbing epistemology and ontology with the realism of phenomenology will further the aims of a feminist film theory.

There has been much insight in feminist writing into the issues centering around cinematic representation and feminist issues that, if disentangled from its expression in terms of idealism/nominalism, may serve the aims of feminist film theory most effectively.

One way in which the rather short history of feminist film theory may be written involves two differing phases. In a first phase, there was interest in exposing the images of women in film history. It was found that such images tend to diminish the possibility of women realizing their potential, to establish deleterious role models for women, and to support an already entrenched patriarchal order. Occasionally somewhat more productive images were discovered; for instance, for Molly Haskell:

Any criticism of [Ingmar] Bergman must be prefaced with the understanding that he, more than any other director and in movies that were a revelation for their time, took women seriously, looked with curiosity and respect at every facet of their lives...never thought of them as second-class citizens (the reverse, if anything...)[1]

(For others, it should be noted, Bergman has been thought a misogynist.) All too often, a woman is depicted as easily accepting relationships in which she is subordinate to a man, sacrificing career and self-development for husband and child while conceiving of self as passive, emotional, intuitive, and nurturing in opposition to being an active, rational agent in the affairs of the world outside the home.

Thus, a question for this first phase of feminist film theory had to do with whether and how the image of a woman in a given film reflected or distorted the reality of women's condition in the society in which the film was made. In addition, there was the assumption that stereotypical images of women contributed to women accepting their lot; given the power of the movies to reinforce, cultivate, even install role models, it was thought that advances in women's consciousness raising about their condition would be made by realization of the distorted image of women to which they are exposed.

This first phase in feminist film theory gradually became supplanted by a second phase, one inspired and formed by the development of poststructuralism. Second-phase feminist film theory shifts the focus of analysis in certain crucial ways. First-phase feminist film theory was rejected in second-phase feminist film theory partly because it was thought that the former asks questions that reflect naivete.

To ask, "Do images of women in film reflect women's nature and condition?" makes assumptions that second-phase feminist film theory does
not want to make. It assumes that there is a reality of women's condition and nature existing independently of film against which an assessment may be made as to faithfulness or distortion.

Christine Gledhill, for example, argues that feminist film theory may
escape "the trap of regarding films as reflections, faithful or distorted,
of society."[2] In writing on this segue from a first to second phase,
Gledhill notes that:

Concentration on characters and stereotypes has been displaced by the se-
miotic/structuralist concern with "textural production," on the grounds that we
cannot understand or change sexist images of women for progressive ones
without considering how the operations of narrative, genre, lighting, mise-en-
scène, etc., work to construct such images and their meaning.[3]

The directions in which feminist film theory has developed are quite
complicated with many variations issuing from this initial dissatisfac-
tion with the terms in which women in cinema are put. To appreciate
feminist film theory as it has evolved, it is important to understand
some of the main strands in the conceptualization of representation
underlying the theory.

Christine Gledhill has called for a realist epistemology for feminism:

If a radical ideology, such as feminism, is to be defined as a means of providing a framework for political action, one must finally put one's finger on the
scales, enter some kind of realist epistemology.[4]

Turning our attention first to her insightful discussion of issues in
feminist film theory will bring out many of the important issues in
feminism and theory of cinematic representation. The formative influence of idealist/nominalist framework may be seen to lend confusion
where clarity would be provided by the realist framework.

Gledhill valorizes a move to a metalevel vis-à-vis the real for any development of a feminist theory of cinematic representation. In the following passage, she argues for this metalevel investigation as a
necessary step in realizing feminist goals:

Before a proper mode of representation or aesthetic relation to the "real" can
be established, we have to have some idea of where the "real" itself is located,
and how, if at all, we can have knowledge of it. At issue then is the status of
"lived experience," of phenomenal appearances, their relation to underlying
structures, the determining role of "signification" in production of the real,
and the place of "consciousness in this production."[5]

Gledhill puts "real" in quotes in conformity with the contemporary film theoretical approach to questions of knowledge, wherein it is problematic whether the term "real" has a referent. For Gledhill, a crucial relationship is thought to exist between "phenomenal appearances" and the real. To decide where the real is, and to decide whether we can have knowledge of it, we must start with phenomenal appearances.

Gledhill assumes that signification plays a determining role in the production of the real, with consciousness playing a constitutive role in such production.[6] With respect to signification, we find that "what the audience at a film recognizes as real is not an unmediated reality about the product of socially formed codes."[7]

To speak of the determining role of significance in production of the real and the place of consciousness in this production involves a misunderstanding of the nature of mediation occurring in the act of recognizing what an art object represents. Phenomenology provides an account of representation in which we are enabled to notice both subject and object in the act of cognition/perception. We come to realize, via the method of reduction, how the noemata mediate the act of consciousness in grasping the object represented. Subjectivity codetermines the noemata but cannot, as Gledhill thinks it can, determine the nature of *the* object of the act.

Moreover, the role of signification is nil with respect to the nature of the real. The object represented by an art object is unaffected by the language we use to describe it. Though the language we use affects the noemata and plays a role in subjectivity's codetermination of the noemata, we cannot make an object represented in a work of art different simply by the language we use to describe it.

Gledhill and other feminist film theorists want the term 'woman' to be a term in a language with a merely language-relative status, not a term with a referent. Mary Ann Doane contends that the female spectator exists "nowhere but as an effect of discourse."[8] Cinema is conceived as a kind of discourse rather than as an object perceived by an independently existing spectator. The terms 'female' and 'femininity' are not taken as referring to "actual members of a cinema audience."[9] Apparently the idea is that a term like 'female' is a merely arbitrarily grounded classificatory term that, though useful in certain circumstances, has no referent. Gledhill elaborates that the category "women" should be the focus of analysis, not "woman." In recognizing gender position in terms of group membership – that is the category women – as opposed to the patriarchal "woman" according to Gledhill "is precisely to leave behind an individual identification and begin to recast the self in terms of a group membership."[10]

Teresa de Lauretis shares the view that women and images of

women have a discourse-relative status. It is her aim to confront "theoretical discourses and expressive practices (cinema, language, narrat-
ing, imaging) which construct and effect a certain representation of
'woman.' "[11] She makes a familiar feminist film theoretical move by
proposing that:

By "woman" I mean a fictional construct, a distillate from diverse but congruent discourses dominant in Western cultures . . . which works as both their
vanishing point and their specific condition of existence.[12]

We come to see that by 'woman' she has in mind "the other-from-
man [nature and mother] site of sexuality and masculine desire, sign
and object of men's social exchange." She contrasts 'woman' with
'women,' where the latter are "the real historical beings who cannot as
yet be defined outside of those discursive formations but whose material existence is nonetheless certain."

In spite of what Gledhill and others in feminist film theory may say,
the terms 'woman' and 'man' do have referents. Biological theories
serve as grounds for making differentiations between women and men,
between woman and man, along familiar lines – differences in repro-
ductive organs and roles, differences in physical capacities. That the
biological theories change from time to time while always remaining
subject to revision has to do with the fallibility of human knowledge
not with there being no referents for these terms. The generalizations
that we use to describe a woman apply to all women but are true only
with a certain degree of probability. The lack of certainty about these
generalizations has nothing to do with the claim to universality that
all such scientific generalizations make.

From its inception feminist film theory has been ambivalent about
issues surrounding the nature of women. Whether or not to acknowledge gender difference is at the heart of the ambivalence. Acknowledging gender difference is thought to be at the root of social inequalities
that have given rise to feminist film theory. As the argument goes, so
long as patriarchal culture has an excuse, in the form of gender differences, for saying that men can do things that women cannot, unjustified economic and social inequalities will persist. If men and women
were not so differentiated in their portrayal in film (and television), it
would not be so easy to discriminate in favor of men in the guise of
simply acknowledging inherent strengths, weaknesses, and so forth.
With the motion picture medium being one of the most powerful forces
in the life of our society, images of women that acknowledge gender
difference will only exacerbate an already unjust situation.

On the other hand, there seem to be compelling reasons for acknowledging gender difference. Only with a recognition of what it is to

be feminine in this culture and the nature of female spectatorship (and male spectatorship, too, e.g., the oft-mentioned woman as object of the male gaze) can feminist film theory expose the perturbing situation and seek to ameliorate by fostering an alternate feminist film practice/criticism.

Laura Mulvey has played a central role in an effort to conceptualize spectatorship of images of women in the motion picture. Her approach derives from certain concepts in psychoanalysis and semiotics. Her "Visual Pleasure and Narrative Cinema"[13] has been a classic in feminist film theory. Though she subsequently revised her account[14] in an effort to trace female spectatorship more adequately, her original article has to be considered in any assessment of feminist film theory and will be our focus.

For Mulvey, the female form in classic Hollywood cinema exists to be seen. The film unfolds so as to invite scopophilic pleasure on the part of the male viewer: Point of view editing strategies that are used by the classic style foster male identification with male characters who exercise the gaze on the female characters in the film. Sequences are staged, blocked, paced, photographed, and edited in order to facilitate women being taken as objects of the male gaze.[15] It seemed from Mulvey's analysis that the male gaze was imposed upon female spectators as well as fostered in male spectators.

Mulvey elaborates upon woman as the object of the male gaze to add that the presence of the female form introduces the complication that its appearance arouses castration anxiety in the male spectator.[16] Where being the object of the male gaze might offer the prospect of unadulterated pleasure for the male spectator, Mulvey points to an edge to the experience; the sight of the woman's body arouses male awareness of woman's lack of a penis provoking the castration anxiety. In order for classic Hollywood film to foster visual pleasure while mitigating the castration anxiety potential of its representations, certain strategies are employed, that is, fetishism and voyeurism.[17] The female form, for instance, may be utilized as an object of fetishist desire, for example – as in the elaborate visual compositions surrounding von Sternberg's portrayal of Marlene Dietrich characters (e.g., *Blonde Venus*). Hitchcock films provide an exemplar supposedly of voyeuristic strategy, containing the castration threat while activating the male gaze phenomenon. For instance, under this analysis, it may be thought that in *Vertigo* we are led to identify with a voyeuristic Scotty who remakes women characters into objects of the male gaze while reducing their castrating threat potential.

Mulvey wants to utilize the Lacanian/Althusserian framework to criticize the classic film as patriarchal in its manner of positioning spectators. Her contention was that classic film positions the male as bearer of the look while the female is consigned to being the object of the gaze. Spectatorship, under this analysis, comes to be regarded as masculinized even for the female viewer. In response to criticisms that female spectatorship can only be conceptualized as an absence under her approach, Mulvey has produced a reading and theoretical analysis of *Duel in the Sun* intended to make proper room for the female spectator. According to Mulvey, the female spectator "enjoying the freedom of action and control over the diegetic world that identification with the male hero provides, gains access to repressed material" (ADS, 29). Mulvey argues that one aspect of Freud's theory shows that in woman-centered film experiences, classic films arouse a kind of identification that has become second nature for woman to respond to in terms of a transsexual identification.[18] Mulvey wants to use *Duel in the Sun* to illustrate how a particular Freudian theory of identification would illumine a film wherein a woman character is central to the story. The film does not posit an active hero and a passive, posed woman heroine existing to be an object of the male gaze. It is rather an "interior drama of a girl caught between two conflicting desires – oscillation between 'passive' femininity and regressive 'masculinity' " (ADS, 35). Mulvey analyzes the female character in terms of semiology:

Woman is no longer the signifier of sexuality.... Now the female presence as centre allows the story to be actually, overtly, about sexuality; it becomes a melodrama. (ADS, 35)

In a vivid passage, Mulvey takes as her focus "a woman central protagonist [who] is shown to be unable to achieve a stable sexual identity, torn between the deep blue sea of passive femininity and the devil of regressive masculinity" (ADS, 30). The female character Pearl in *Duel in the Sun* embodies oppositional features of the two male characters, Leut and Jesse. With Leut, the oedipal dimension is reactivated while Jesse "signposts the correct path for Pearl, towards learning a passive sexuality, ... sublimation into a concept sexuality that is socially viable" (ADS, 35). Ultimately, there is no room for Pearl in either Jesse's or Leut's worlds.

Mulvey wants to argue that *Duel* exemplifies that women spectators' identification with the masculine in its phallic aspect reactivates "a fantasy of action that correct femininity demands should be repressed" (ADS, 37). Under Mulvey's analysis, Pearl's position in *Duel* is similar to that of the female spectator as she temporarily accepts "masculinization" in memory of her "active" phase. This female indulgence in a fantasy of masculinization is at cross purposes with what society expects of her.[19]

Mulvey's original view of spectatorship and representations of women and men in film is not justifiable for a variety of reasons. Mulvey's picture of male characters in classic cinema as active while female counterparts are passive, serving primarily as "objects" to be seen, admits of telling counterinstances. Many male stars have been presented as objects of erotic attention. One thinks of the actors who played the various incarnations of Tarzan – Johnny Weismuller, Buster Crabbe, and so forth. One thinks also of the Steve Reeves epic vehicles as well as contemporary films showing off the physiques of the likes of Arnold Schwarzenegger. There are even genres centrally devoted to creating visual pleasure by exposing male physical attractiveness via photographic and editing practices – for example, boxing films. Action is slowed down, and lighting and camera angles conspire in countless films to show off the good looks of major male film stars (e.g., Gable, Fonda, Brando).

Moreover, the idea that female characters are passive, merely there to be the objects of glamorous close-ups and erotic full shots is belied by the history of classic film. Marlene Dietrich, for instance, was often a controller, not a mere object of the gaze. In no way may the film performances of Bette Davis, Joan Crawford, Katharine Hepburn – major actresses of classic cinema – be fixed with the image of the passive, posed figure. In addition, as Gaylin Studlar has pointed out, a masochistic aesthetic modeled after Deleuze may be more plausibly used to model spectatorship of the von Sternberg–Dietrich collaborations than the male gaze formula that Mulvey finds so attractive.[20]

Also, as discussed in an earlier section, the reference to the castration anxiety central to Mulvey's account introduces implausibilities that further weaken her theory. There seems little reason to suppose that cinema spectatorship involves either fetishism or voyeurism in the robust senses of those terms that Mulvey's theory requires. Fetishism and voyeurism are perversions arising in special circumstances, not characteristics of the average cinemagoer. They involve regression and fixation in archaic stages of development characteristic of only a very small portion of the potential moviegoing population. If Mulvey is merely using "voyeurism" in a popular sense to mean that cinema spectators often like to see cinema characters in a circumstance wherein they, the spectators, are not seen, she is probably correct, but no psychoanalytic grounding for her account of spectatorship would be involved, as she wishes it to be. If she insists on psychoanalytic grounding for her account, then she is clearly extending voyeurism and fetishism beyond their proper psychoanalytic uses, rendering her account of cinematic representations of women unjustified.

Moreover, with respect to voyeurism, Noel Carroll has put it well:

The idea of voyeurism as a model for all film viewing does not suit the data. Voyeurs require unwary victims for their intrusive gaze. Films are made to be seen and film actors willingly put themselves on display, and the viewers know this. Mulvey claims that the conventions of Hollywood film give the spectators the illusion of looking on a private world. But what can the operative force of "private" be here.[21]

With recognition of the deficiencies in an account of spectatorship such as that provided by Mulvey, the ambivalence about whether to acknowledge or deny gender difference remains an issue to be addressed.

Gledhill recognizes this ambivalence in feminist film theory in the following passage:

The spectator of "essentialism," especially problematic for feminism where the whole question of gender definition is so loaded, compounds the post-structuralist refusal of representation and identification. Assertion of our social difference – maternity, feeling, irrationality – seems only to make patriarchal equations: woman as earth-mother, woman as other. On the other hand, constructions of our culture-heroines as strong and powerful bring charges of male identification or substitution. We seem trapped. However we try to cast our potential feminine identifications, all available positions are already constructed from the place of the patriarchal other so as to repress our "real" difference.[22]

These concerns of feminist film theorists about gender difference are real ones. They should not, however, be conflated with theorizing about the nature of cinematic representation, especially about the term "woman" having no referent. There is no reason why feminist film theory cannot opt for acknowledging gender difference. Identifying differences between men and women need not lead to patterns of discrimination though, of course, they can be an excuse for such patterns occurring. There is a deeper reason as well for the value in acknowledging gender difference. Underlying so much of what is valuable in feminist film theory is an implicit contrast between what women really are as opposed to their false portrayal in the film medium. For instance, Teresa de Lauretis regards feminism as a political intervention; she argues persuasively for a needed sensitivity to representation of women in cinema as follows:

The representation of woman as spectacle – body to be looked at, place of sexuality, and object of desire – so pervasive in our culture, finds in narrative cinema its most complex expression and widest circulation.[23]

Such a description has a ring of truth about it because we already have justified beliefs about characteristics of women in life outside their portrayal in movies; such knowledge permits criticism of media portrayals of women as false to their true condition.

On another related issue, Gledhill contends that feminist appropriation of recent film theory reveals the problematics involved in exposing the potential to oppress and the sheer falsity of filmic images of women; she argues that attempting to replace such images with reality and truth is fraught with difficulty. First, defining the reality of women so as to counteract distortion is not easily done. Feminist analysis is necessary in order to achieve such a counteraction, a mode of analysis *inaccessible* to many.[24] Second, stereotypes are a part of our reality. "Realism narrowly defined in terms of actuality is not a powerful enough weapon to disengage women's fantasy from its imbrication in consumerist structures."[25] Third, realism can preserve rather than challenge the status quo: "A naturalist ideology proposes that Reality equals what we see ... and that the camera offers a window on the world, therefore cannot lie."[26] Gledhill points out that "naturalism not only ignores the filmmaking apparatus but also the fact that the iconic sign is caught up in other signifying systems – linguistic, aesthetic, social, fictional, etc., – which together structure the film."[27] Gledhill, however, questions whether a theory of realism "should equate all varieties of realist practice with the goal of naturalism."[28]

With phenomenology as grounds for a realist theory of cinematic representation, one may deal with this cluster of problematics that Gledhill identifies. As discussed earlier, the reality of women is discoverable (with horizon analysis in mind). It is no more difficult to discover truths about women than it is with respect to any other entities, that is men, events, objects, or states of affairs. If a feminist analysis were to acknowledge the existence of women independently of their representation in the motion picture, with the means of discovering truths about women in society no different than in any other circumstance, no issue of inaccessibility to women who are oppressed and/or falsely characterized would obtain. It is adoption of the idealist/nominalist framework that leads to this issue of knowledge of woman or women, not anything intrinsic to the nature of women, men, culture, society, or life.

As noted, there are at least two notions of realism: One is stylistic, the other epistemological. Gledhill is apparently conflating the two when she discusses how stereotypes are part of our reality. Isn't it true that we appreciate what feminist writing has been saying about women in film being objects of the male gaze because we have knowledge of women independently of their depiction and portrayal in the media? We know that women's life potential is vastly richer than such representation in classic cinema has shown it to be. Stereotypes exist in our culture. If Gledhill is merely marking this fact by saying that stereotypes are part of our reality, no one could argue with her. It would seem clear, however, that she means more: she wants to say that stereotypes are inextricably bound up with our apprehension of reality such that we cannot know truths about women independently of their representation in our culture. Once we realize that women's fantasy and every other feature of our manner of apprehension of anything including women extends only to the noema and does not extend to the object of cognition/perception, we realize that there is no reason to think that we cannot know truths about women's condition in society.

Gledhill is correct in questioning a so-called naturalist framework, with its naive realist base; we have discussed before the unfruitfulness of offering a choice between naive realism and the kind of idealism/nominalism at the basis of poststructuralism instead of being concerned about the difference between phenomenology and idealism/nominalism. The reference she makes to the iconic sign being caught up in other signifying systems, which together structure the film, does not constitute a problem for phenomenology. To hold a realist view about cinematic representation is not to posit realist depictions/portrayals as expressed in iconic signs. Quite the contrary, the hyletic data that together with the operations of the noema/noesis *guide* our perception to an apprehension of women as the entities represented by the motion picture need not be iconic at all. There can be distortions of all sorts in depictions of women; there can be highly abstract portrayals of a woman with virtually no visual similarities obtaining. A woman may indeed by symbolized by a particular motion picture sequence even though no woman is realistically portrayed in the sequence. For example, the character Rebecca in Hitchcock's *Rebecca* is symbolized by the letter *R,* but we see no actress on screen playing Rebecca. Her presence is felt throughout the film though no relation of iconicity is involved.

From this, it should be clear that phenomenology may be utilized fruitfully to pursue feminist objectives. It is, of course, the argument of this book that Husserlian phenomenology, with its realist grounding, will serve this purpose. As Frank Tomasulo has pointed out (and as was pointed out in the Introduction to this work), the term 'phenomenology' has been used in film theoretical writing in ways that diverge dramatically from the intent of its founder. As Tomasulo puts it:

Phenomenology is neither a subjective enterprise nor an objective one, neither an idealism nor a vulgar materialism, although it has been presented in all these guises.[29]

Gaylyn Studlar has attempted to delineate ways in which phenomenology may be a means for better conceptualizing feminist film theory.[30] Her effort is salutory; unfortunately, however, she is hampered by some of the misconceived notions of the nature of phenomenology. She starts by ascribing features to phenomenology that the method could not have:

Phenomenology and feminism are rarely associated.... The reasons for this disjunction are strikingly obvious at first glance. The former stands as a paragon of male philosophical observation. The latter proclaims its interest in transforming an oppressive system rather than being content with interpreting it. (RFP, 69)

To support this characterization of phenomenology as male philosophical observation, Studlar quotes Marx's comment from "Theses on Feuerbach": "The philosophers have only interpreted the world in various ways; the point however, is to change it" (RFP, 77n1).[31] What we see as Husserl's effort to develop a method for recognizing the nature and activities of subject and object at the same time in the act of cognition, Studlar takes to be a method for positioning the self as a passive acceptor of the world.[32] She quotes Dudley Andrew on an alleged "rightism" of phenomenology since phenomenologists are "anxious to change nothing but instead to comprehend a process which flows along perfectly well on its own" (RFP, 70–1).[33]

She also quotes Husserl from the *Cartesian Meditations* to the effect that "the phenomenological ego becomes a disinterested onlooker above the naively interested ego" (RFP, 70; *CM*, 35). She then alleges that.

the differences between men and women in a Husserlian *Labenswelt*, the moving historical field of our lived experience, are inconsequential to the phenomenological quest – the quest for the origin of meaning, for the transcendental essence (eidos) to be discovered in the meeting of consciousness: subject and object. (RFP, 71)[34]

Thus, the method of reduction in Husserl is sexist in its failure to acknowledge gender difference, such failure or acknowledgment being a typically male approach.

Instead of carefully attending to the development of Husserl's epistemological theories from its earliest moments, as has been done here, and understanding what the kind of inquiry epistemology involves, Studlar selectively quotes from a few scattered passages in later Husserl and interpreters such as Maurice Natanson,[35] Ludwig Binswanger, and Dudley Andrew while attributing to Husserl's epistemological theorizing characteristics it cannot have. No interpretations of Husserl can be done without taking into account the development of his thought. No characterization of his philosophical reflection as sexist can be made on a partial explication of his thought.

As we have seen, to *bracket* the natural standpoint cannot in any way be characterized as sexist in that it involves a failure to acknowledge gender difference. To use the reduction is to refrain from *describing* the act of cognition in terms of assumptions of the natural standpoint. It has nothing to do with either recognizing or failing to recognize differences between men and women. With respect to a purported passivity or status as a disinterested onlooker being the subjects' positioning via Husserlian phenomenology, there can be no basis in Husserl for such an interpretation. As we have seen, the method of reduction reveals that the self (as is true of *the* object of perception) exists independently of the act of cognition. No inference may be drawn about what type of political action the self is inclined to engage in or refrain from, be interested in or be disinterested in. There is indeed no incompatibility between Husserl's epistemology and any form of political philosophy or any political action. There is also no connection between utilizing the phenomenological, transcendental, and/or eidetic reductions and any political stance whether it be rightist, leftist, or centrist. Further, it can be true as Marx says in "Thesis on Feuerbach" that the point is to change the world not merely to interpret it, and for one who wants to change the world to use the method of reduction. Using the method does not involve putting the world aside, becoming uninterested in it, or refraining from being involved in it. Studlar fails to recognize that the reduction has to do with refraining from *describing* phenomena in terms of assumptions of the natural standpoint. The world remains quite unaffected by the act of bracketing. It is not ignored; the observer is not either passive or active; the possibilities for amelioration are not attenuated even in the slightest degree. Husserl's extensive discussion of the reduction in *Ideas* (§31) makes clear the nature of the method.

Despite these misinterpretations of phenomenology, Studlar does seek some common terrain that phenomenology and feminism can mutually explore. She says:

Nevertheless, instead of discarding phenomenology as a pipedream of pretended neutrality or dismissing it as a methodological anachronism in which only men can afford to indulge, we should search for the ways in which feminism can appropriate phenomenology. (RFP, 71)

Her effort toward reconciliation of phenomenology and feminism involves drawing the distinction between first- and second-phase feminist film theory, noting the move from analysis of images of woman to textual production.[36] She then indicates that we need a "reading against the grain" – criticism with attention to textual gaps, fissures, contradictions, and incoherences – as strategy for "immersion in a cinema structured for male pleasure and catering to patriarchal needs" (RFP, 72). Such a textual archeology would seem antithetical to Husserl's dictum: "back to the things themselves." But she argues that "even within a theoretical climate that distrusts things and much prefers to affirm the power of signs" Husserl's dictum is not as alien to second-phase feminism theory as it sounds.[37] The common ground she finds between the two theoretical approaches has to do with setting aside (making "strange") naive notions of reality before moving to a neutral description of the immediacy of experience.[38]

Instead of interpreting Husserlian realism as compatible with contemporary feminist film theories, Studlar would do better to acknowledge the irreducibility of the two epistemologies – Husserl's and that of feminist film theory, with its unacknowledged, perhaps unrecognized, commitment to an idealist/nominalist framework.

Studlar instead wants to proceed to Merleau-Ponty's movement away from Husserl to form an idealist version of phenomenology.[39] It is clear also that Studlar has not really found any significant common ground with what she prefers to think of as "pure philosophical phenomenology." As she says:

The gendered differences in lived experience and in the power relations of discourse make it impossible for feminists to be "good sports" and hold our political claim for women in abeyance while... we perceive simply the cruel radiance of what is. (RFP, 72)

What Studlar and feminist film theorists in general cannot recognize is that the goals of feminism have been tied to an idealism/nominalism with considerable deficiencies but need not be so connected. Indeed, Christine Gledhill's call for some grounding in a realist epistemology is a bright spot in feminist film theory. To go back to the things themselves, in the context of a Husserlian phenomenological feminism, would be to return to woman as woman, which contemporary feminist theorists want. The term 'things' in Husserl's theory carries no sexist connotations. It means object or event or person (whether male or female) or state of affairs existing independently of the act of cognition. Such a return to woman as woman as independently existing would further the feminist project.

Notes

An oriental mode of cinematic representation

1. Noel Burch, *To the Distant Observer: Form and Meaning in the Japanese*

Cinema (Berkeley: University of California Press, 1979); hereafter abbreviated *TDO*.

2. On facture, see Michael Renov, "Re-Thinking The Documentary: Towards A Taxonomy of Mediation," *Wide Angle,* 8(3–4), 75.

Cinematic sound

1. Elizabeth Weis and John Belton, *Film Sound: Theory and Practice* (New York: Columbia University Press, 1985).

2. Mary Ann Doane, "Ideology and the Practice of Sound Editing and Mixing," in Weis and Belton, *Film Sound,* pp. 54–62, and "The Voice in the Cinema: The Articulation of Body and Space," in Weis and Belton, *Film Sound,* pp. 162–76.

3. Doane, "The Voice in the Cinema," p. 163.

4. Jean-Louis Baudry, "Ideological Effects of the Basic Cinematographic Apparatus," in Nichols, *Movies and Methods, Vol. II* (Berkeley: University of California Press, 1985).

5. Ibid., p. 532.

6. Doane, "Voice in the Cinema," p. 162. The term 'fantasmatic' originated in Daniel Doyan's article "The Tudor Code of Classical Cinema," in Nichols, *Movies and Methods, Vol. I* (Berkeley: University of California Press, 1976), pp. 438–50, esp. p. 443.

7. Ibid., p. 167.

8. Ibid., p. 162.

9. Ibid.

10. Ibid., p. 172.

11. Ibid., p. 166.

12. Christian Metz, "Aural Objects," in Weis and Belton, *Film Sound,* pp. 154–61.

13. Ibid., pp. 156–7.

14. Ibid., p. 157.

15. Ibid., p. 158.

16. Ibid., p. 159.

17. Ibid.

18. Ibid., p. 161, note 7.

19. Bill Rothman, "Against the System of the Suture," in Bill Nichols, *Movies and Methods, Vol. I* (Berkeley: University of California Press, 1976), pp. 451–68.

20. Kaja Silverman, "Dis-Embodying the Female Voice," in Mary Ann Doane, Patricia Mellencamp, and Linda Williams, *Re-Vision: Essays in Feminist Film Criticism* (Los Angeles: AFI, 1984), pp. 131–49.

21. Ibid., p. 131.

22. Ibid.

23. Ibid., p. 132.

24. Ibid.

25. Ibid.

26. Ibid., p. 131.

27. Ibid.

The fabula

1. David Bordwell, *Ozu and the Poetics of Cinema* (Princeton: Princeton University Press, 1989); hereafter abbreviated *OPC*.
2. David Bordwell, *Narration in the Fiction Film* (Madison: University of Wisconsin Press, 1985) and David Bordwell, Janet Staiger, and Kristen Thompson, *The Classical Hollywood Cinema: Film Style and Mode of Production to 1960* (New York: Columbia University Press, 1985).
3. In Aristotle, *De Poetica*, in Richard McKeon, *The Basic Works of Aristotle* (New York: Random House, 1941), p. 1455.
4. Bordwell, *Ozu and Poetics*; all quotes in this paragraph from p. 176.

The diegesis

1. David Bordwell, *Ozu and the Poetics of Cinema* (Princeton: Princeton University Press, 1989), pp. 51–2.
2. Noel Burch, *To the Distant Observer: Form and Meaning in the Japanese Cinema* (Berkeley: University of California Press, 1979); abbreviated *TDO*.
3. Ibid., p. 19.
4. Etienne Souriau, *L'universe filmique* (Paris: Vrin, 1953), Preface, p. 7; "La structure de l'universe filmique et le vocabularie de la filmologie," in *Revue Internationale de Filmologie*, 7–8, 231–40.
5. Christian Metz, *Film Language, A Semiotics of the Cinema*, trans. Michael Taylor (New York: Oxford, 1974), pp. 97–8.
6. Bill Nichols, *Ideology and the Image: Social Representation in Cinema and Other Media* (Bloomington: Indiana University Press, 1981), pp. 317–18.
7. Ibid.
8. Ibid., p. 184.
9. Edward Branigan, "Diegesis and Authorship in Film," *I.R.I.S.* (Fall) 1989, 3.
10. Ibid.
11. Ibid., p. 2.
12. Ibid., pp. 3–4.
13. Ibid., p. 4.
14. On the meaning of the term *psychic distance* in aesthetics and the distinction between psychic and emotional distance, see Allan Casebier, "The Concept of Aesthetic Distance," *Personalist* (Winter) 1971, 70–91.

The Imaginary

1. Jacques Lacan, "The Mirror stage as formative function of the I as revealed in psychoanalytic experience," in Lacan's *Ecrits* (New York: Norton, 1977), pp. 1–8.
2. Christian Metz, *The Imaginary Signifier: Psychoanalysis and the Cinema*, trans. Celia Britten, Annwyl Williams, Ben Brewster, and Alfred Guzzetti (Bloomington: Indiana University Press, 1977), see esp. chaps. 3 and 4.
3. Noel Carroll, *Mystifying Movies: Fads and Fallacies in Contemporary Film Theory* (New York: Columbia University Press, 1988), p. 63.

4. Rick Altman, "Psychoanalysis and Cinema," in Bill Nichols (ed.), *Movies and Methods, Vol. II* (Berkeley: University of California Press, 1985), pp. 519–20. Originally appeared in *Quarterly Review of Film Studies,* 2(3) (August 1977). Reprinted courtesy Harwood Academic Publishers GmbH.
5. Lacan, "The Mirror stage," p. 2.
6. On the relationships between the Imaginary and the Symbolic in Lacan's theory, see J. LaPlanche and J-B. Pontalis, *The Language of Psychoanalysis,* trans. D. Nicholson-Smith (New York: Norton, 1973) under the headings "Imaginary" and "Symbolic."
7. Ferdinand de Saussure, *Course in General Linguistics,* trans. Wade Baskin (New York: Fontana-Collins, 1974).
8. Rich Altman, "Psychoanalysis and Cinema," p. 518.
9. Christian Metz, *Imaginary Signifier,* p. 74.
10. Noel Carroll, *Mystifying Movies,* pp. 64–5.
11. Ibid., pp. 65–6.
12. Ibid., p. 66.
13. Richard Wollheim, "The Cabinet of Dr. Lacan," *New York Review of Books,* 25 (21–22), January 25, 1979.
14. Ibid., p. 43.
15. Ibid., pp. 43–4.
16. Ibid., p. 44.
17. Carroll, *Mystifying Movies,* pp. 42–3.

Feminist theories of cinematic representation

1. Molly Haskell, *From Reverence to Rape: Treatment of Women in the Movies,* 3rd ed. (Baltimore: Penguin, 1974), p. 315.
2. Christine Gledhill, "Developments in Feminist Film Theory," in Mary Ann Doane, Patricia Mellencamp, and Linda Williams (eds.), *Re-Vision: Essays in Feminist Film Criticism* (Los Angeles: AFI, 1984), p. 19. All quotes from this work are reprinted by permission of Greenwood Publishing Group, Inc. © 1984.
3. Ibid.
4. Ibid., p. 41.
5. Ibid., p. 20.
6. Ibid.
7. Ibid., p. 23
8. Mary Ann Doane, *The Desire to Desire: The Woman's Film of the 1940's* (Bloomington: Indiana University Press, 1987), p. 20.
9. Ibid.
10. Gledhill, "Feminist Film Theory," p. 26.
11. Teresa de Lauretis, *Alice Doesn't: Feminism, Semiotics, Cinema* (Bloomington: University of Indiana Press, 1984), p. 5.
12. Ibid.; this and the quotes in the following paragraph are from p. 5.
13. Laura Mulvey, "Visual Pleasure and Narrative Cinema," *Screen,* 16(3) (Autumn 1977), 6–18.
14. Laura Mulvey, "Afterthoughts...Inspired by *Duel in the Sun," Framework,* Nos. 15–17 (1981). The article (hereafter ADS) has been reproduced in a col-

lection of her essays entitled *Visual and Other Pleasures* (Bloomington: Indiana University Press, 1989). All page references to this article herein will refer to the latter source.

15. Mulvey, "Visual Pleasure and Narrative Cinema," pp. 8–13.
16. Ibid., p. 8.
17. Ibid., pp. 13–14.
18. Mulvey, "Afterthoughts," p. 33.
19. Ibid., p. 37.
20. Gaylin Studlar, "Masochism and the Perverse Pleasures of the Cinema," *Quarterly Review of Film Studies*, 9(4) (Fall 1984), 267–82.
21. Noel Carroll, "The Image of Women in Film: A Defense of a Paradigm," annual meeting, American Philosophical Association, Los Angeles, 1990, p. 6. For a useful criticism of Mulvey's "Afterthoughts," see Miriam Hansen, "Pleasure, Ambivalence, Identification: Valentino and Female Spectatorship," *Cinema Journal*, 25(4) (Summer 1986), 6–29.
22. Gledhill, "Feminist Film Theory," p. 28.
23. de Lauretis, *Alice Doesn't*, p. 4.
24. Gledhill, "Feminist Film Theory," p. 21.
25. Ibid.
26. Ibid., pp. 21–2.
27. Ibid., p. 22.
28. Ibid.
29. Frank Tomasulo, "The Text-in-the-Spectator: The Role of Phenomenology in an Eclectic Theoretical Methodology," *Journal of Film and Video*, 40(2) (Spring 1988), 20.
30. Gaylin Studlar, "Reconciling Feminism and Phenomenology: Notes on Problems and Possibilities, Texts and Contexts," *Quarterly Review of Film and Video*, 12(3) (July 1990) (hereafter RFP). All quotes © Harwood Academic Publishers Gmbh.
31. The Marx quote is referred to in Frederick Engels, *Ludwig Feuerbach* (New York: International Publishers, 1935), p. 75. Studlar indicates that she is reworking the quote in posing this contrast between phenomenology and feminism.
32. Studlar, "Reconciling Feminism," p. 70.
33. The Andrew quote is from "The Neglected Tradition of Phenomenology in Film Theory," in Nichols, *Movies and Methods, II*, pp. 625–32.
34. She relies on Ludwig Binswanger, *Being-in-the-World*, trans. Jacob Needelman (New York: Basic Books, 1963) for this interpretation.
35. Studlar, "Reconciling Feminism," p. 69. Maurice Natanson, *Edmund Husserl, Studies in Phenomenology and Existential Philosophy Series* (Evanston: Northwestern University Press, 1973), p. 19.
36. Studlar, "Reconciling Feminism," p. 72.
37. Ibid.
38. Ibid.
39. Ibid.

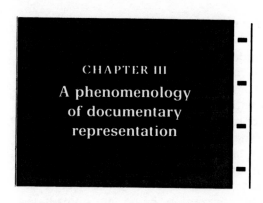

CHAPTER III

A phenomenology of documentary representation

In contemporary theory and practice of the documentary film, embrace of the idealist/nominalist theory of cinematic representation has led to questions about the legitimacy of the documentary form itself. Such writing draws upon the ontological and epistemological assumptions of idealism/nominalism, with sometimes an admixture of the philosophical theories of Jacques Derrida. (The use of Derridean theory will be the focus of a later section.) At the same time, antidocumentary filmmaking seeks to undermine the conditions governing expression in the documentary genre by the way in which the film is made; the filmmakers seek to foster spectator skepticism about the belief that a documentary film may have a referent. (Analysis of *Sans soleil* later in the text will be illustrative.) In the next section, attention will be turned toward conceptualizing the documentary and measuring idealist/nominalist analysis against that of phenomenology.

Rescuing the documentary

Two impossible identities often propose themselves for our consent in documentary and ethnographic film. (1) What you see is what there was. (2) What there was is what there would have been.   – Bill Nichols[1]

Bill Nichols draws upon the distinction between unmediated and mediated perception, which we see as unuseful in analyzing perception. Here he uses the distinction in talking about two assumptions that have often been made in thinking about the documentary. Nichols says that "the first proposition – 'What you see is what there was' – invites us to believe that our access to the pro-filmic event is complete and unmediated."[2] In the theory of the documentary, the term *profilmic* refers to the event the documentary is about in its relation to the camera or other aspects of the cinematic apparatus.

As discussed earlier, no viable epistemology, including that of phenomenology, rests upon a conceiving of perception as unmediated.

The issue is not whether perception is unmediated or mediated but rather what kind of mediation is involved. As we have seen, phenomenology posits a most sophisticated account of mediation. Nichols's analysis involves four elements with a restricted notion of their possible matchings: unmediated and mediate are one pairing; discovery and construction are the other. The arguments developed in this work substantiate that perception may be both a discovery and a mediated process. For Nichols, to the contrary, the notion of the perceiver of a documentary as a discoverer not a constructor of the object represented can only be paired with perception being an unmediated process.

In the discussion of horizon, it was pointed out that it is the nature of perception that no object (whether designated as profilmic or whatever) is such that our access to it is *complete*. Accordingly, it does not follow from our access to an event being always mediated and always incomplete that "what you see is what there was." Indeed, as we have seen for phenomenology, a standard case of film perception involves an apprehension of events, whether past or present, where perception is mediated and the object appears to us in incomplete form. In the *Shoeshine* (*Sciuscia*) illustration, post–World War II Italian life is apprehended as one of the objects represented by the de Sica film. The mediation and incompleteness of the object as it appears to us in no way precluded post–World War II Italian life being apprehended as it was.

Toward a taxonomy of mediation in documentary experience

While much fiction stakes a ... claim via the much-discussed "illusion of reality," only the documentary foreswears (realism) for a direct, ontological claim to the "real."   — Michael Renov[3]

Renov wants to show that this claim by the documentary entails "a metaphysics of presence which denies the concrete and historical interventions which are the constituent elements of all social practices."[4] *Presence* is a key term in Renov's characterization of the documentary claim. (We shall discuss Derrida's concept of presence in the next section.) Here we consider the idea of the referent of the documentary *being present* in the experience of the documentary. When an object is present in a film experience, it turns out that the object is *in* the experience, as it is in itself, not even modified by the conditions of reception and by cinematography, editing, and other aspects of cinema. As argued earlier, phenomenology never proposes; in fact, it disclaims, a notion that the object is *in* the experience. What appears to us in film experience *guides* perception to an independently existing object; it is not the case that in the documentary, the object enters experience unaffected by the operations of the cinematic apparatus and our manner of reception. It does not enter experience; the noemata mediate its apprehension and are codetermined by subject and object.

Renov seeks to establish that the apparatus and conditions of reception alter the object "documented" such that what we see is not what was there. He quotes Raymond Williams to the effect that "all active relations between different kinds of being and consciousness are inevitably mediated."[5] He notes that contemporary film theorists have tended to "stress the notion of signifying practices, discrete activities which produce meaning within an historical framework."[6] Renov distinguishes four sites where mediation occurs, transforming the object of the documentary film: the historically real, the profilmic, the text, and the spectator. He anticipates his argument as follows:

At each juncture of this relational sequence, the naturalized or immediate continuity of elements must be interrogated with the result that the documentary film, once thought to be a semi-permeable membrane that connected the spectator to the world becomes a deliberately confected presentation of selected material photographed, recorded and arranged in a precise way, experienced by a precise audience at a particular moment of history via a specific mode of transmission.[7]

Echoes of the Bazinian model of cinematic realism are evident in metaphors such as documentary film being a "semi-permeable membrane." As noted in the discussion of the epistemology of cinematic representation, one can be a realist about cinematic representation yet reject the image of cinematic experience as one where the spectator looks through a "window" or other transparant entity to see the things themselves, without any mediation by self or circumstance.

The first two sites in Renov's taxonomy of mediated instances in the experience of the documentary may be abandoned in favor of the referent, the object depicted or portrayed or symbolized by the film. The historically real and the profilmic are distinguishable only on an idealist/nominalist model. The profilmic refers to the object in relation to the view of the camera; the historical real[8] refers to the object as it exists independent of any relationship to the cinematic apparatus or cinematic spectatorship. There is no reason to distinguish these two with respect to the object depicted or portrayed or symbolized by a documentary. There is a referent, which may or may not be affected by the presence of the camera depending on the particular circumstances. Nichols's question is an important one – "Is what was there what would have been there?" The answer has no essentialist answer such as Renov and Nichols want to give. There is nothing about a camera showing an object that necessitates that that object cannot be known by spectators who subsequently apprehend it via an experience of the documentary made about it. This is not to say that there are not cases where the presence of the camera may intrude upon the "natural responses" of individuals who are the subjects of documentaries such that we would incline toward saying that what you see in the documentary was not what you would have seen had the camera not been present. It all depends on contextual factors occurring during the shooting, not any essential factors of the experience process.

Identifying the documentary

Prior to an application of phenomenological analysis to the process of mediation in the documentary experience, it will be useful to clarify the nature of this nonfiction medium. In characterizing the nonfiction film, as we can see from the preceding quotes, there has been a desire to historicize the documentary form. In an important article, Carl Plantinga attempts to systematize this effort with an assimilation of nonfiction filmmaking to the model of a speech act. Plantinga argues that the opposition between fiction and nonfiction film is

a function of two broad and opposed functions of discourse in every society. The opposition, however, should not be grounded in any textual properties the documentary or the fiction film may have. Instead, the documentary or fictional nature of texts grounded in the "stance" of the text's producer(s) and on an implicit contract between producer/author and the viewer/reader to view or read the work according to certain conventions.[9]

Plantinga explains that documentary filmmakers take a different kind of stance in terms of what their films are about than do fiction filmmakers. Documentary filmmakers take an assertive or interrogative stance, whereas "the typical stance taken by the artist of fiction is the fictive stance."[10] When one takes a fictive stance, the audience is *invited* to consider the state of affairs portrayed; the documentary asserts that the state of affairs occurred or interrogates whether it did or did not occur.

Michael Renov discusses the assertive stance of the documentarist in terms of truth-claim:

Every documentary issues a "truth-claim" of a sort, positing a relationship to history which exceeds the analogical status of its fictional counterpart.[11]

In an associated idea, Noel Carroll characterizes the documentary in terms of indexing:

Non-fiction films are those that we evaluate on the basis of their knowledge claims in accordance with the objective standards appropriate to their subject-matter. Producers, writers, directors, distributors, and exhibitors index their films as non-fiction. We don't characteristically go to films about which we must guess whether they are fiction or non-fiction.[12]

The documentary is, thus, to be viewed as making a truth-claim and is indexed as the kind of film that issues the truth-claim. Plantinga goes on to model the documentary in a further way – on a quasi-contract basis. He tells us that:

I have merely described what I take to be a major requirement viewers and producers currently make of documentaries in order that the *implicit contract* to view a work as documentary might be honored.[13]

The legal notion of defeasibility may be useful in explicating this further requirement for being a documentary.[14]

It is characteristic of defeasible concepts that we cannot state sufficient conditions for their application, such as a determination of whether a contract has been made. This is so because there is an open list of defeating conditions any one of which can rule out application of the concept. In the case of a contract, for instance, offer and acceptance only count toward the assumption that a valid contract exists; there are also defeating conditions that can appear in certain circumstances to override offer and acceptance, for example, fraudulent misrepresentation, duress, lunacy, and so forth.

With respect to the documentary we may hold that a kind of tacit agreement or quasi-contract holds between production/distribution and viewers governed in the manner of defeasibility. The indexing/assertive stance view by itself, however, makes it look too much like there are simply two types of film, nonfiction and fiction films, whose different status has its locus in purely conventionally grounded characteristics of the film and its publicity; in fact, knowledge independent of the features of our film experience and the publicity attendant to the film's distribution is crucial, that is, our knowledge of the object documented, the nature of intentional consciousness, and our perceptual act's horizon are additional and important features in any adequate account of the nature of a documentary.

Some illustrative examples of documentaries will serve to bring out characteristics of the documentary experience: Shinsuke Ogawa's *Heta Village (Heta buraku)*, William Wyler's *Memphis Belle*, Jean Rouch and Edgar Morin's *Chronique d'un été*, and Nick McDonald's *The Liberal War* (1972).

In analyzing Ogawa's *Heta Village (Heta buraku)* and Tsuchimoto's

Minamata: The Victims of the World (*Minamata: Kanja-sans to sono sekai*), Joan Mellen offers the following perspective:

Among their virtues, these documentaries [Ogawa and Tsuchimoto] don't pretend to be objective.... [They] see their films primarily as political acts designed to strengthen the determination of the peasants who are their subjects to resist the giant conglomerate Zaibutsu.[15]

Heta Village

Ogawa's *Sanrizuka* (of which *Heta Village* is part) is a documentary series about the efforts of peasants to resist the Japanese government's (ultimately successful) efforts to build the Narita International Airport on their land in the 1970s.

Ogawa's cameras capture peasant resistance as it in reality occurred in the early 1970s in Japan. The peasants are seen in Ogawa's film as they actually resisted governmental efforts to build the airport. Objectivity in the documentary would consist in accurately showing the peasants' resistance efforts.

To posit the actions of the peasants as an existing referent for the film and to allow for an objective cinematic rendering is, as discussed earlier for contemporary film theory, too simple and unsophisticated a conceptual framework. For contemporary theory/criticism, when a filmmaker shows a peasant revolt, such as that against the Narita airport, it is thought crucial to realize that the filmmakers are only providing spectators with a *representation* of the revolt. This is so partly because the filmmakers' subjectivity inevitably obtrudes upon an effort to show any event (attitudes, biases, feelings, beliefs, etc.). This is so partly because the limitations of the cinematic medium prevent accurate rendering of any event (the distortion provided by lens, framing, etc., excludes part of any event, changes the look of any event, etc.). This is so partly because the presence of the cinematic apparatus alters the actions/reactions of those performing actions/reactions before the camera (individuals behave differently when they know a camera is running than if they do not). This is so partly because there is no such entity as a referent that exists independently that a camera could capture; such a referent would have all of its properties independent of spectator inscription in the text, which theory excludes as a possibility, as explained earlier.

Accordingly we find Mellen praising the *Sanrizuka* series for not even *pretending* to be objective. While the film was being shot, daily rushes were shown to the peasants.[16] Dialogue between peasants and filmmakers ensued in a way that acknowledged a supposed constructedness essential to the filmic effort but denied "the pretense" of the traditional documentary (e.g., sometimes Ogawa was castigated by the peasants for the way he filmed their actions). The filmmaker Ogawa did not aim to be an objective observer showing the revolt in as un-biased a way as he could; rather as Mellen puts it: "Documentarist Shinsuke Ogawa completely identified himself with [this] struggle."[17] There is little effort to impose order or instill interest where the struggle has none. Ogawa's "search" is for authenticity and the flavor of the struggle rather than for falsely imposed Aristotelian unities, dramatic climaxes, and easy resolutions"[18]

Heta Village is indeed an important case for any theory of the documentary to take into account. Its peculiarities, as noted, do not, however, sustain an idealist/nominalist model of documentary representation.

In delineating the nature of our documentary film experience, two enterprises need to be kept distinct. Though it may be true that no documentary can fully portray its referent because of the filmmaker's subjectivity, and it may be a fact that the film medium will inevitably leave something out or distort the appearance of it due to built-in limitations of the medium, these considerations have nothing to do with whether the film is or is not a documentary. *Heta Village* is a limited vision of the resistance due to features of the film medium, filmmaker, and reception, but it is a documentary nevertheless. Ogawa seems to have sought (as Mellen points out) the flavor of the struggle rather than imposing unities on the action where there were none. Ogawa invited input from the documentary's subjects as part of the filmmaking process. None of these features precludes the film from being a documentary or providing an objective rendering of the peasant protest. Objectivity is a matter of degree, not an absolute condition. It is not possible to fully document an event such as the peasant resistance, but this fact does not entail that a useful distinction cannot be made between objective and subjective renderings of the resistance any more than the presence of the camera precludes a distinction between non-fiction and fiction films.

Memphis Belle *and* The Liberal War

Wyler's *Memphis Belle* will serve to illustrate a realist account of documentary representation. In this World War II documentary, the crew of an airplane, named *Memphis Belle,* is followed from start to finish through the bombing of a key German installation at the German city of Wilhelmshaven. Cameras mounted on the plane provide views of takeoff, flight to the destination, flight over the target, release of bombs by the bombardier, attack by enemy planes, and the flight to home base.

The referent of the documentary is the event – the bombing run – including the smaller events enumerated. The sensa that the audience experiences guide perception to that bombing run. The sensa are not part of the bombing run; the bombing run does not enter into spectators' experience at a screening of the documentary. The bombing run is an actual event that existed independent of the Wyler documentary and spectators' perceptual acts in apprehending it. A long take does not comprise the documentary. Instead we are provided with views at tarmac level of the bomber's wheels leaving the surface on takeoff for the mission, the approaching sights of Wilhelmshaven, shots of the bombardier pressing the bomb-dropping device, sights of the bombs falling, views of enemy planes at 3 o'clock, and so forth.

Experience of these sensa, objects, and events guide our perception to grasp the bombing run event; they do not offer sensa out of which the spectator constructs the bombing run event, as the idealist epistemology would have it. Our perception is constrained to be guided to the bombing run; it is not free to take in the sensa and then construct a bombing run or construct something else if we so wish. A phenomenology of the experience of the Wyler documentary would reveal the constraints and deny the idealist freedom to construct the object of the documentary.

How very different than *Memphis Belle* is another film, Nick McDonald's *The Liberal War,* which, though a film about a war, too, the Vietnam conflict, leaves the lens capped on that war. Reference to the Vietnam war is made by a combination of narration and shots of bric-a-brac from someone's living room. We are given not scenes of soldiers, battle, bombing, refugees, and so forth but models of the conflict made out of toy soldiers, newspapers, coins, bottles, dominoes, and so forth. In one sequence, the difficulty of extricating American troops is illustrated by toy soldiers trapped in a narrow-necked bottle; in another sequence, the domino theory – if Vietnam falls, all of the other Southeast Asian countries will fall like dominoes – is illustrated by actual dominoes; in still another sequence, American financial interests in the war are represented by coins on a map of Vietnam.

Memphis Belle is a documentary about war in a way *The Liberal War* is not. The latter is a film essay about the war. It is not a documentary about a war. The hyletic data with which it bombards the subject and the noemata codetermined by object (and subject) are unconnected with the referent in a way they are not for the Wyler film. Narratives, film essays, and documentaries all have a capacity to guide us to real-life referents. Nick McDonald's film may guide our perception to a real event, a real war, just as much as Wyler's film guides us to another real event, another war, an event in World War II. The way the Wyler film codetermines the noemata is that of a documentary. The way McDonald's film codetermines the noemata is nonfictional but not documentary. Part of what it is to be a filmic documentary is to take and use motion pictures of the referent.

As we shall see in the case of *Chronique d'un été*, there is no reason to distinguish the historically real from the profilmic. All of the distinctions that Nichols wants to bring out with his questions – "Is what you see what was there?" and "Is what was there what would have been there?" – may be explicated with the notions of referent and documentary representation no matter how complex the referent of the documentary, no matter how ironic the manner of portrayal, no matter how self-reflexive the style; the distinction between historically real and profilmic need not be made. The object, event, or persons before the camera are a referent that may or may not be faithfully portrayed, whatever else the documentary may seek to accomplish (the Rouch and Morin film has other objectives).

Chronique d'un été

Chronique d'un été, Jean Rouch and Edgar Morin is a self-reflexive documentary. It not only is about the process of documenting a subject (hence reflexive), but it also is about the process of mediation involved in reception of the documentary (hence self-reflexive – it is about the self's encounter with cinema).

The film has several aspects. It presents two young women walking around Paris with a microphone, putting questions like "Are you happy?" to passersby on the street and registering the reactions. An interview with one of the interviewers precedes her interrogating activity. The film records her reflections on the possible interventions that the cinematic apparatus may have upon her in an interview.

The film also shows discussions by Rouch and Morin about the activity they are engaged in, that is, making this very documentary. There are also collective discussions about documentary filmmaking. Rouch also at times is his own cameraman. Mike Eaton comments upon this reflexive aspect of several Rouch films:

Any audience that the [Rouch] films construct must, it would seem, be complicit in taking on trust that Rouch knows what to film and when to film it... because Rouch is thus posed as "the first viewer" (through the viewfinder of his camera) and the "first editor" (by deciding when to pull the trigger on his camera) of his films, his relationship to editors, when he uses them, becomes very specific. For Rouch the editor is not someone whose job is to construct coherence from the mass of raw footage he has shot. That has been achieved already by Rouch himself, editing in the camera as he shoots.[19]

In another sequence in *Chronique*, Rouch has participants in the documentary as audience of the film. The penultimate sequence of the film records the reactions of the participants who have just seen the rushes.

Rouch has made it clear that, though the released print of *Chronique* bears the subtitle "An Experiment in Cinema Vérité," he never meant the film to capture reality directly. Rouch preferred to describe his film work in terms of it being accomplished with *his presence.* He knew many of the people filmed. Accretions of trust between Rouch and the people filmed could lead to their revealing themselves and their discomfort in the presence of the apparatus through the medium of Rouch and his camera. Rouch says the following:

There is a whole series of intermediaries and these are lying intermediaries. We contract time, we extend it, we choose an angle for the shot, we deform the people we're shooting, we speed things up and follow one movement to the detriment of another movement. So there is a whole work of lies. But, for me and Edgar Morin at the time we made that film this lie was more real than the truth. That is to say, there are a certain number of things happening, human facts surrounding us...which people would not be able to say any other way ...It's a sort of catalyst which allows us to reveal, with doubts, a fictional part of all of us, but which for me is the most real part of an individual.[20]

If the unwanted framework of documentary as a presentation of an unmediated reality is put aside and is replaced by the phenomenological framework of a mediation by spectators via the noema/noesis/horizon, the elaborate reflexity and self-reflexivity, the distortions that Rouch points to, the undoubted problematic of the presence of the camera, and so on may be seen to provide no theoretical ground for calling the legitimacy of the documentary into question. Acknowledging the ways in which these aspects may inhibit spectator apprehension of the objects of Rouch's film in no way entails that the film did not have a referent or that it did not document that referent.

The passersby on Paris streets had attitudes, beliefs, intentions, and desires related to whether they were happy or not. When asked "Are you happy?" by the aggressive interviewers, it does not matter that several of them avoided responding to the question. To document a person's attitude via a motion picture does not require that the effort succeed, that the attitude be revealed, that it be truthfully told. The noemata that were provided in the interviews reach out to the attitude sought. An intentional direction was given to the sensa. The context, as discussed earlier, mobilized horizons associated with documentary to constrain spectator experience. The assertive stance, the indexing, and the discussion with the interviewer prior to engaging in the interviews in the street scenes serves to constrain perception to an actually existing referent – attitudes about their own happiness at that time – not to fictional content.

The reflexive and self-reflexive aspects of *Chronique* merely complicate the apprehension. They make the process of making this very documentary a referent of the film in addition to the attitudes of Parisians as referent. A compound referent including self-reflexivity is just as much a referent as one without this aspect. The status of documentary, even the documentary status of the very film that one experiences, exists independently of the sensa and mediating noema/noesis just as much as the attitudes of Parisians do. That our apprehension of any of these referents is obtruded upon by the deliberate revelation of the presence of the cinematic apparatus and the mediations involved in reception has nothing to do with there being actually existing referents for the Rouch–Morin film.

Summary

The foregoing conceptual observations and documentary illustrations establish the advantages of a phenomenological account of the documentary form. In order to analyze the experience of the documentary properly, all we need are the phenomenological categories; in documentary experience, we apprehend a motion picture that has a referent that consciousness, with its intentionality and its mediating horizons and noemata, is able to grasp. There is no need to question the legitimacy of the genre due to an alleged misguided ontological claim to the real. The acknowledged presence of subjectivity in filmmaker and spectator activity constitutes no barrier to documentation of a referent as the proper aim of the genre. The presence of self-reflexivity in some of the most creative films made in the genre is in no way inconsistent with portrayal of an independently existing referent as a primary goal of documentaries.

It remains to consider what problematics for the theory of the documentary may arise when Derridean deconstruction is brought to bear on the endeavor to understand the nature of the experience of a documentary.

Derridean deconstruction and the documentary

Interjection of Derridean deconstruction into the theory of the documentary brings with it difficulties of an even deeper variety than have so far been encountered with the idealist/nominalist conceptualization of the genre. Jacques Derrida has proposed a critique of a supposed Western metaphysical tradition that he characterizes as "logocentric" – "logos" for the Greeks stood for reason and logic.[1] As such, the Western philosophical tradition has emphasized rationality and logic.

Derrida proposes a corrective for logocentrism that has come to be known by the term *deconstruction*. The meaning of the term may be explained in terms of what it is not as well as in terms of what it is. It is not metaphysics, that is, proceeding via reason, logic, philosophy; it is not dialectics as with Hegel; it is not Husserlian phenomenology; it is not a critique of pure reason as with Kant.

On the positive side, though deconstruction is not metaphysics, it depends on and utilizes its conceptual apparati. Under the name "metaphysics," there resides, for Derrida, truth, logic, reason, and philosophy, all modes of analysis, interpretation, and understanding. Derrida has called metaphysics the "logos that believes itself to be its own father."[2] By this he means that metaphysics has an origin external to itself but the enterprise has disconnected itself from this origin. It is this past that Derrida seeks to uncover. In disclosing the origin of metaphysics, Derrida believes he will be disclosing the condition for the possibility of metaphysics itself. The search for the origins of metaphysics is not a historical one. It has its locus rather in reading metaphysics in another way. Derrida claims to find "presence" at the heart of metaphysics. Presence as central to metaphysics was, according to Derrida, inaugurated by the pre-Socratic Greek philosopher Parmenides. In her commentary on Derrida, Irene Harvey explains Derrida's sense of the notion of presence:

From Parmenides to Husserl "the privilege of the present as evidence" is an essential trait in the history of metaphysics. In Husserl's return to the things themselves... we must remember that the basis of this claim was a metaphysical "prejudice" for the locus of truth in the pure presence of the things themselves to consciousness.[3]

For Derrida, presence has been the condition of the possibility and ultimate criterion for evidence and truth. Making things themselves present to consciousness is an idea that Derrida seeks to deconstruct. The antedote for presence is to be found in *differance*. The term *differance* is a combination of the terms *differer* (to differ) and *deferer* (to defer). The word *differance* is not to be thought of in terms of the technical sense of a term. It is neither a name nor a concept. Words such as *dissemination, trace,* and *archi-trace* may be used just as well as *differance*. Of this family of words of deconstruction, each serves as well as any other to further the deconstructive activity. Nevertheless, *differance* is the most well-known "marque" of this family. Derrida discusses *differance* in relation to presence as follows:

Differance in its active movement – what is comprehended in the concept of difference without exhausting it – is what not only precedes metaphysics but also extends beyond the thought of being (of presence). The latter speaks nothing other than metaphysics, even if it exceeds it and thinks it as what it is within its closure.[4]

Differance is probably best rendered in English as "differing." Derrida wants to emphasize movement and process, which he finds overlooked in the concept of presence, with its static conception of things being present to consciousness when we know them. Derrida is interested in how, in consciousness, things are not characterized by presence but by extension, deferment, substitution, iteration, repetition, oscillation, and so forth.

Derrida explains that the "name of differance" is not a proper name. With respect to *differance* being a process, Derrida says:

Older than Being itself, such a differance has no name in our language. But we "already know" that if it is unnameable it is not tentative because our language has not yet found or received this name or because it is necessary to search in another language, outside the finite system of ours. It is because there is no name for that – not even essence or Being, not even that of "differance" which is not a name, which is not a pure nominal unity and dislocates itself ceaselessly in a differing chain of substitution.[5]

Deconstructionism aims to limit metaphysics not destroy it. In doing so, it leaves a track in the text. Insofar as it leaves such a track, there has been a deconstruction of metaphysics. The track is not something that comes into being because of the deconstructive activity; it has always been there but is revealed by deconstruction. With respect to how deconstruction borrows, for example, the resources of metaphysics in its deconstructive activity, Derrida says the following:

The movements of deconstruction do not destroy structures from the outside. They are not possible nor can they take accurate aim except by inhabiting those structures. Inhabiting them in a certain way...operating necessarily from the inside, borrowing all the strategic and economic resources of subversion from the old structure, borrowing them structurally that is to say without being able to isolate their elements and atoms, the enterprise of deconstruction always in a certain way falls prey to its own work.[6]

Deconstruction takes more than one form. In considering how a deconstruction of the documentary form may take place, one considers deconstruction as a dealing with texts. In such a "transaction," deconstruction is not an interpretation. It is rather a consideration of a text as a congeries of signs. Deconstruction activity looks at signs as signs, not at signs as signifiers of a signified in a system of reference.

It also involves a consideration of rhetorical figures within a text (synechdoche, metonymy, etc.).

In addition, the deconstruction activity shows how, with respect to the meaning and representation in a text that, for whatever seems plausible to say, a reader can always say the opposite. The point is not, however, to elicit ambiguity, but rather to urge the perspective that texts do not have any determinate meaning.[7]

Once having considered texts as sets of signs in those ways, deconstruction does certain things with the texts. It shows how in texts as complexes of signs, some structure is at work that prevents decidability about the meaning and representation of the texts. Under deconstructive analysis, things are not what they seemed prior to the deconstructive activity. The deconstructive activity accomplishes the bringing about of this perspective by transacting with the text in a way that renders the text a subverter of itself.

Ecriture, *presence, pretense*

An ideal case for understanding the relevance of Derridean deconstruction for conceptualizing the documentary form is Chris Marker's *Sans soleil*:

> *Sans soleil* fully embraces [a] flight from identity and presence toward a logic of the supplement both at the level of narrated language and of the structuring of sound and image.[8]

This Derridean perspective on Chris Marker's film may well be fruitful given Marker's conversance with the climate of opinion prevailing at the time in which the film was formulated and filmed. Not only may Derridean theory provide a useful conceptual map of the extraordinary twists and turns of the landscape in Marker's film but undoubtedly Derrida has been a considerable force in the development of the intellectual zeitgeist of the 1970s and 1980s.

With Jacques Derrida's assault upon a supposed Western metaphysical tradition as interpretive vehicle, *Sans soleil* becomes not a documentary about an experience of Japan but an artistic embodiment of a critique of the documentary form itself, as traditionally conceived, a critique promulgated along lines analogous to and consonant with Derridean deconstruction of logocentrism. Under this interpretation, *Sans soleil* is regarded as a deconstruction of the documentary form, that kind of film that aims to show spectators a referent. (In the case of *Sans soleil*, Japan would be an obvious candidate for referent, or we may say "aspects of Japanese culture and society.")

In Renov's conceptual mapping of *Sans soleil* in terms of Derridean deconstruction, he characterizes documentary utterance as "originary or iterative," a status that precludes a referent having *presence* for us. *Sans soleil* accordingly is taken as divorced from "the dream of presence over signifying practice," while having been made independent of a condition wherein there is a "unification of sign and referent."[9]

The picture we are to have of the traditional documentarist versus the deconstructionist Marker is that the former seeks to provide the experience of presence of the referent to the spectators while the latter knows that only the supplementary may be produced.

Sans soleil, under this interpretation, is to be regarded as "writing" in the honorific sense – *écriture.* As the theory goes, once we appreciate the implications of Derrida's exposure of the logocentric roots of Western metaphysics, we come to valorize a certain approach to enunciation (in whatever form the enunciation obtains). *Ecriture* is "inherently mediate," it has a secondarized status in that it has supplementarity as a crucial feature, and it acknowledges trace structure as the proper concern of those who engage in expression. To recognize that presence is an unattainable goal and that *écriture* is the favored mode of expression, it is important to cognize language as a process of interweaving:

No element can function as a sign without referring to another element which itself is not simply present. This interweaving results in each element ... being constituted on the basis of the trace within it of the other elements of the chain or system.[10]

Thus, nothing is ever simply present or absent; "there are only everywhere differences and traces of traces."[11] Elements accordingly are eliminated in favor of traces, with language then being only a set of institutional traces and all expression in language becoming writing, supplements arising in a chain of differential references.

It is no wonder that under Derridean-inspired analysis the documentary has no referent that the filmmakers can make present for spectators. If acts of enunciation, whether in philosophy or literature or cinema, are always and only about themselves, transcendence of the act of expression to a referent cannot obtain. When representational capacity is exposed as illusory, all enunciation becomes trace and deferment.

Mediation is certainly prominently displayed in *Sans soleil.* The film is at once a film about Japan, a film about the nature of filmmaking, about remembrance and forgetting, and about the making of history. The film purports to be a record of the experience of an individual named Sandor Krasna, a fictional construction, whose letters are conveyed to the audience by a nameless woman narrator through whom further filtering occurs (in respect of her style of delivery, her tone of voice, her reactions to the letters, etc.). The filmmaker does not utilize his real name but a mediating name, Chris Maker. Late in the film, a perspective from a far distant time is used as further mediating structure:

An impossible tale [a film tale is told] of a time-traveler from the year 4001 who has lost not his memory but his power to forget. . . . [This] film which can only be imagined lends its title to the text that has absorbed it, installing it as a kind of global referent for itself.[12]

Moreover, the film seems to express a mediated consciousness of Japan, connecting an experience of Japan in the 1980s with events, artifacts, and events to which it is externally related – revolution in Guinea-Bissau, memories of the look of Iceland, Hitchcock's *Vertigo,* impressionistic landscapes of the Ile de France, as well as political/cultural happenings deemed important by some consciousness occurring since Marker's 1965 film *The Koumiko Mystery* (*Le Mystère Koumiko*).

At the end of *Sans soleil*, the woman narrator asks poignantly, "Will there be a last letter?" raising the issue of totalizing: It is basic to logocentrism, according to Derrida, that a totalizing potential to experience exists that may be countered by supplementarity. Enunciation is always open: It can never come to a unified ending; closure and unity are mere pretenses foisted on us by logocentrism.

The deconstructive aspect that one finds in the Marker film is not necessarily incompatible with the film documenting a referent, for example, certain aspects of Japanese culture. In experiencing *Sans soleil,* our perception is at many times guided to features of late-twentieth century Japan. We are given views of a culture existing simultaneously as hypertechnological and primitive throwback, as a media-saturated society whose inhabitants also live according to ancient Shinto and Buddhist religious matrices, for example, rituals according reverence for broken dolls and debris are presented for our observation.

In experiencing these documentary aspects of *Sans soleil,* our perception is constrained by the hyletic data with which the film bombards us and by horizons associated with the documenting of culture and of the nature of cultural practices. We do not have a choice to have our reaching out to the referent Japan attenuated by the deconstructive thrust of the film, a feature that Renov quite plausibly argues is present in the Marker film.

The idealist/nominalist framework for conceptualizing the documentary experience would posit an incompatibility between recognizing the deconstructive aspect and the documenting of Japan. Under this analysis, as we have seen, spectators really only encounter hyletic data, which they then construct into a meaningful form. The force of the intervention of the deconstructive activity would be determinative of the structure lent to the text by spectators, squeezing out the choice of structuring the sensa into documentary form.

Since, however, perception of a film is always intentional, involving a reaching out to independently existing objects – Japan being a primary referent and the documentary form as traditionally conceived being a referent – spectators are not in a position of choosing what are their objects of perception. In the case of *Sans soleil,* they apprehend both some aspects of Japanese culture and are subject to the subversive deconstructive activity that Marker has enacted.

The deconstructive activity must be conceptualized with the idealist/nominalist framework underlying. Marker's film *aims* to deconstruct the documentary form. To believe that deconstruction can obtain is founded upon an acceptance of the idealist/nominalist framework, which, as we have seen, has most burdensome conceptual deficiencies. Were contemporary film theory and filmmakers such as Marker to realize how deeply problematic the idealist/nominalist framework is, their inclinations toward embracing deconstructive activity would surely be attenuated if not canceled. To generate deconstruction as a plausible way of dealing with a film (or a way of creating a film) requires conceptualizing a film as a set of signs governed by codes, introducing hyletic data into the experience of spectators at a site (the screening of a film) where spectator activity creates a text; deconstruction is a process for once having found trace, *differance,* and so forth in the text so created to subvert the text from within. The roots in idealism/nominalism should be apparent. Take away these epistemological and ontological grounds for identifying the film and deconstruction goes, too. Given that a film is not to be conceptualized in the ways that deconstruction needs, there is reason to hold that a filmmaker like Marker has aimed to deconstruct the documentary with *Sans soleil* and critics have aimed to deconstruct texts but they cannot succeed. It only seems that filmmaker and critic are deconstructing because of the attachment and unquestioning acceptance of the idealist/ nominalist framework.

Notes

Rescuing the documentary

  1. Bill Nichols, *Ideology and the Image: Social Representation in Cinema and Other Media* (Bloomington: Indiana University Press, 1981), p. 241.
  2. Ibid.
  3. Michael Renov, "Re-thinking Documentary: The Truth of the Text." *Wide Angle,* 8 (3/4), (1986): 71.

4. Ibid., p. 72.
5. Ibid., quoting from Raymond Williams, *Marxism and Literature* (Oxford: Oxford University Press, 1977), p. 98.
6. Renov, "Re-thinking Documentary," p. 72.
7. Ibid.
8. Ibid., p. 73.
9. Carl Plantinga, "Defining Documentary: Fiction, Non-Fiction, and Projected Worlds." *Persistence of Vision* (5, Spring 1987), 46.
10. Ibid.
11. Renov, "Re-Thinking Documentary," p. 71.
12. Noel Carroll, "From Reel to Real: Entangled in the Non-Fiction Film." *Philosophical Exchange*, (14, 1983), 24.
13. Plantinga, "Defining Documentary," p. 50; italics added.
14. On defeasibility, see H. L. A. Hart, "The Ascription of Responsibility and Rights," in *Logic and Language, First Series* (Oxford: Blackwells, 1951).
15. Joan Mellen, *Waves at Genji's Door: Japan Through Its Films* (New York: Pantheon, 1976), p. 248.
16. Ibid., p. 429.
17. Ibid., p. 433.
18. Ibid.
19. Mike Eaton, "The Production of Cinematic Reality," *Studies in the Anthropology of Visual Communication*, 6 (2). (Summer, 1980), 44–45.
20. Jean Rouch, "Les Aventures d'un nègre blanc," interview with Jean Rouch by Philippe Esnault, *Image et Son*, no. 249, April 1971.

Derridean deconstruction and the documentary

1. Jacques Derrida, *Of Gramatology*, trans. Gayatri C. Spivak (Baltimore: Johns Hopkins University Press, 1974), pp. 3 and 24.
2. See Derrida's essay "Eperons: 'Les Styles de Nietzche,'" trans. Barbara Harlow (Chicago: University of Chicago Press, 1978).
3. Irene Harvey, *Derrida and the Economy of Differance* (Bloomington: Indiana University Press, 1986), p. 104.
4. Derrida, *Of Gramatology*, p. 143.
5. Derrida, *Marges de la Philosophy* (Paris: Editions de Minuit, 1972), p. 28.
6. Derrida, *Of Gramatology*, p. 24.
7. Jacques Derrida, "Le Facteur de la vérité," in *The Postcard: From Socrates to Freud and Beyond,* trans. Alan Bass (Chicago: University of Chicago Press, 1987), esp. pp. 411–18.
8. Michael Renov, "Documentary/Technology/Immediacy: Strategies of Resistance," Annual Meeting, University Film and Video Association, Loyola-Marymount University, August 6, 1987, p. 5.
9. All quotations ibid.
10. Jacques Derrida, *Positions* (Chicago: University of Chicago Press, 1981), p. 26.
11. Renov, "Documentary/Technology/Immediacy."
12. Ibid.

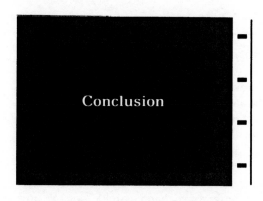

Conclusion

We have seen that a phenomenological account of the experience of cinematic representation provides a picture wherein spectators are discoverers of the objects represented by the motion picture. Their apprehension is mediated by the noema and the noesis; horizons constrain the noemata that serve this mediating function. Subject and object codetermine the nature of these noemata. Though the object represented remains unaffected by the activities of the knowing mind, subjectivity plays a crucial role in bringing about the mediating noemata/noeses. The noemata are apperceived not perceived. In performing the reduction, we may realize the role of the noemata mediating apprehension of *the* object of perception, the represented object. In the act of apprehending representations, consciousness is intentional, that is, it reaches out to independently existing objects. Intuition, in the form explained by Husserl, is the faculty or disposition that spectators utilize in apprehending the object of the perceptual act. The function of the critics in writing about cinematic representation consists in using the resources of language to activate spectators' intuitions to grasp what they, the critics, have grasped in the motion picture.

In addition, in apprehending cinematic representations, spectators recognize the exemplification of universals in what appears to them. This recognition is part of the process of apprehending what the motion picture represents. No generalizations, including codes, govern depiction, portrayal, and/or symbolizing in a motion picture although there are recurring structures, apprehendable by intuition, that contribute to the occurrence of cinematic representations. The processes involved in apprehending cinematic representations are conscious in nature, rather than products of unconscious processes. It is nevertheless true that, in the act of recognizing cinematic representations, spectators are not conscious of some aspects, that is, the noema/noeses; to be nonconscious of such aspects of one's act does not make those aspects unconscious. Finally, the theory of language utilized in the phenomenological account of cinematic representation involves

155

terms having referents; accordingly, the diacritical theory of language is rejected.

How very different is the model prevailing in contemporary film theory with its roots in idealism/nominalism! For advocates of the poststructuralist synthesis, spectators are constructors of the text, contributing to the constitution of the object represented. Acknowledgment of mediation in the act of apprehending cinematic representations precludes the independent existence of the object represented by the motion picture. No distinction is made between apperception and perception. Perception stops with what have been called "sensa" and that Husserl calls "hyletic data." The objects represented are constructions out of these data, with spectators' constructive activity governed by such things as codes. Contemporary film theory functions with a nominalist framework, acknowledged or unacknowledged, that dictates that only particulars exist, in the form of images and sounds; universals do not exist. Whatever general features characterize cinematic representations are in the representations because spectators have constructed them that way not because they are characteristics of the representations.

The underlying theory of language is diacritical. Where phenomenology has intuition as the faculty or disposition that discovers depictions, portrayals, and instances of symbolism, contemporary film theory has tended to posit unconscious processes such as the Imaginary as the source for the construction of representations. For contemporary film theory, with its propensities toward Lacanian psychoanalysis, Althusserian Marxism, and so forth, there is only an individual not a self apprehending representations. The individual has acquired faculties such as the Imaginary as part of a cultural process: The Imaginary is triggered by processes of misrecognition of certain sorts to generate unities in the objects represented by film. It is the constructors of representations, these individuals with only the illusion of identity but no real selves, using culturally relative codes, who constitute cinematic representations.

The concepts of the self issuing from phenomenological and contemporary film theoretical approaches are, therefore, very different. The phenomenological analysis of representation posits a transcendent self; the self exists independently of the introspective acts involved in its apprehension as well as independently of its perceptual acts in grasping representations. It has capacities to see, to hear, to intuit, to reason, to feel. When it apprehends cinematic representations, it does so by means of these capacities. Its apprehension of representations is mediated by the noemata it codetermines. It responds to dispositional properties of the film to affect it in terms of its sensibilities, its prior experiences with art and film, and its capacities to see, hear, intuit, think, and feel. The self exists; it is unified, not in an illusory way, but in an ontologically grounded way.

The phenomenological theory of cinematic representation enables an analysis of important aspects of film experience as well as issues in the relationship between film and society. Cinematic sounds and visuals seem to be not separately experienced phenomena tied together in illusory ways but intentionally related as belonging to real or fictional objects, events, persons, and/or states of affairs. The female voice in cinematic representation is recognized as a property of women as women, that is, women as they are in themselves. The documentary is sustained as a legitimate form of filmmaking activity, providing access to the things themselves. Various hypothesized entities and critical activities of contemporary film theory have been shown to be unnecessary for conceptualizing cinematic representation: an oriental mode of representation, codes, the fabula, the diegesis, the Imaginary, deconstruction. Moreover, a new phenomenological feminist film theory has been proposed. Throughout, the ensnarement of contemporary film theory by the idealist/nominalist framework has been exposed together with indications of the advantages of a phenomenological account of cinematic representation over any representation theory grounded in idealism/nominalism.

Adoption of a phenomenological theory of cinematic representation has important ramifications for film criticism. With a recognition of the independence of the object represented by the motion picture from the activities of the knowing mind (the realist epistemological assumption) and the existence of universals indwelling in the object represented (the realist ontological assumption), the process of critical evaluation may be put in proper perspective. The misplaced value that has been put upon the self-reflexive film can be corrected by a phenomenological perspective with the result that the genre of the self-reflexive film will be recognized to be just another genre, no better or worse aesthetically, politically, or otherwise than any other genre. If perception of a motion picture is not perception of images and sounds alone but of independently existing objects and if there are not just individual things – images and sounds – in our motion picture experience out of which cinematic representations are constructed, films exposing the presence of the cinematic apparatus and bearing the marks of their own inscription will not be overvalued as they have been under the influence of the poststructuralist synthesis.

Correlatively, the documentary and the realist film will not be castigated, as they have been in countless instances of film criticism, for providing an "illusion of reality" or "triggering imaginary unities" where there really are none or making a "claim to the ontologically real" where nonesuch is possible. Rather the cinematic medium may be recognized as having a most valuable capacity to guide spectator perception to the things themselves. As such, cinema is not a hand-maiden to a politically deficient system but one of the many loci of experience facilitating our knowing the world and ourselves.

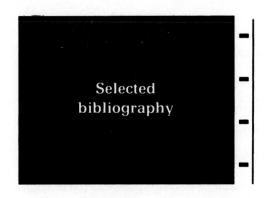

Selected
bibliography

Edmund Husserl

Cartesian Meditations: An Introduction to Phenomenology, trans. Dorion Cairns (The Hague: Nijhoff, 1960). (*CM*)

Crisis of European Sciences and Transcendental Phenomenology: An Introduction to Phenomenological Philosophy, trans. David Carr (Evanston: Northwestern University Press, 1970).

Experience and Judgment: Investigations in a Genealogy of Logic, rev. and ed. Ludwig Landgrebe, trans. J. S. Churchill and Karl Ameriks (Evanston: Northwestern University Press, 1973). (*EJ*)

Husserliana, an ongoing collection of Husserl's works (The Hague: Nijhoff, 1950).

Ideas: General Introduction to Pure Phenomenology, trans. W. R. Boyce Gibson (New York: Collier, 1962) [*Ideen au einer reinen Phänomenologie und Phänomenologischen Philosophie* (Halle: Niemeyer, 1913)]. (*I*)

Logical Investigations, trans. J. N. Findlay (London: Routledge & Kegan Paul; New York: Humanities 1970) [*Logische Untersuchungen* 1st German ed.: (Halle: Niemeyer, 1900); 2nd German ed. (Halle: Niemeyer, 1913/1921)]. (*LI*)

Paris Lectures, trans. Peter Koestenbaum (The Hague: Nijhoff, 1964).

Phenomenology of Internal Time-Consciousness, ed. Martin Heidegger, trans. J. S. Churchill (Bloomington: Indiana University Press, 1964).

"Psychological Studies in the Elements of Logic," trans. Dallas Willard, *The Personalist*, LVIII (October 1977), 297–320 ["Psychologische Studien zur Elementaren Logic," *Philosophische Monatshefte* XXX (1894), 159–91]. (PS)

Commentaries on Husserl

Carr, David. *Interpretive Husserl: Critical and Comparative Studies* (Dordrecht, Netherlands; Boston: Nijhoff, 1987).

Cunningham, Suzanne. *Language and the Phenomenological Reductions of Edmund Husserl* (The Hague: Nijhoff, 1976).

Derrida, Jacques. *Speech and Phenomena and Other Essays on Husserl's Theory of Signs*, trans. David Allison (Evanston: Northwestern University Press, 1973).

Dreyfus, Hubert (ed.). *Husserl, Intentionality and Cognitive Science* (Cambridge, Mass.: MIT Press, 1982).

Elliston, Frederick, and McCormick, Peter. *Husserl: Expositions and Appraisals* (London: University of Notre Dame Press, 1977).

Follesdal, Dagfinn. *Husserl and Frege; ein Beitrag zur Beleuchtang der Entstehung der Phanomenologischen Philosophie* (Oslo: I Kommisjion hos Aschehoug, 1958).

Gurwitsch, Aron. *Field of Consciousness* (Pittsburgh: Duquesne University Press, 1964).

Kaelin, Eugene. *Art and Existence: A Phenomenological Aesthetics* (Lewisburg: Bucknell University Press, 1971).

Miller, Izchak. *Husserl, Perception, and Temporal Awareness* (Cambridge, Mass: MIT Press, 1984).

Mohanty, Jitendranath. *Edmund Husserl's Theory of Meaning* (The Hague: Nijoff, 1976).

—. *Husserl and Frege* (Bloomington: Indiana University Press, 1982).

—. *Transcendental Phenomenology: An Analytic Account* (Oxford: Blackwells, 1989).

Mohanty, Jitendranath, and McKenna, W. *Husserl's Phenomenology: A Textbook* (Washington, D.C.: University Press of America, 1985).

Moreland, James. *Universals, Qualities, and Quality-Instances: A Defense of Realism* (Lanham, Md: University Press of America, 1985).

Ricoeur, Paul. *Husserl: An Analysis of His Phenomenology*, trans. Edward Ballard and Lester Embree (Evanston: Northwestern University Press, 1967).

Smith, David Woodruff, and McIntyre, Ron. *Husserl and Intentionality: A Study of Mind, Meaning, and Language* (Dordrecht, Holland; Boston: Reidel, 1982).

Willard, Dallas. *Logic and the Objectivity of Knowledge* (Athens: Ohio University Press, 1984).

Other phenomenological writings

Dufrenne, Mikel. *Phenomenologie de l'experience esthetique* [in English] (Evanston: Northwestern University Press, 1973).

Heidegger, Martin. *Being and Time*, trans. J. MacQuarrie and E. Robinson (New York: Harper & Row, 1962).

—. *The Essence of Reasons*, trans. Terrence Malik (Evanston: Northwestern University Press, 1969).

Ingarden, Roman. *Ontology of the Work of Art*, trans. Raymond Meyer, with John Goldthwait (Athens: Ohio University Press, 1989).

—. *Poetry, Language, Thought*, trans. Albert Hofstadter (New York: Harper, 1971).

Merleau-Ponty, Maurice. *Phenomenology of Perception* (New York: Humanities, 1962).

—. *Phenomenology, Language, and Sociology: Essays in Honor of Maurice Merleau-Ponty* (London: Heinemann, 1974).

Sartre, Jean-Paul. *Transcendence of the Ego*, trans. Williams and Kirkpatrick (New York: Noonday, 1937).

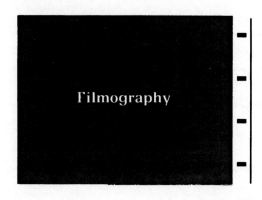

Filmography

Annie Hall, dir. Woody Allen (USA, 1977)

Assassination (Ansatsu), dir. Masahiro Shinoda (Japan, 1964)

Birds, The, dir. Alfred Hitchcock (USA, 1963)

Blonde Venus, dir. Josef von Sternberg (USA, 1933)

Boy (Shonen), dir. Nagisa Oshima (Japan, 1969)

Breathless (A bout de souffle), dir. Jean-Luc Godard (France, 1960)

Ceremony, The (Gishiki), dir. Nagisa Oshima (Japan, 1971)

Chronique d'un été, dir. Jean Rouche and Edgar Morin (French, 1960)

Citizen Kane, dir. Orson Welles (USA, 1941)

Confessions among Actresses (Confession, Theories, Actresses / Kokuhakateki-joyu-ron), dir. Yoshishige Yoshida (Japan, 1970)

Death by Hanging (Koshikei), dir. Nagisa Oshima (Japan, 1968)

Death in Venice (Morte a Venezia), dir. Luchino Visconti (Italy, 1971)

Double Suicide (Shinju ten no Amijima), dir. Masahiro Shinoda (Japan, 1969)

Duel in the Sun, dir. King Vidor (USA, 1946)

Eros Plus Massacre (Eros purass gyakusatsu), dir. Yoshishige Yoshida (Japan, 1970)

He Died after the War ([The Story of] The Man Who Left His Will on Film/ Tokyo senso sengo hiwa), dir. Nagisa Oshima (Japan, 1970)

Heta Village (Heta buraku), dir. Shinsuke Ogawa (Japan, 1972)

In the Realm of the Senses (Ai no corrida), dir. Nagisa Oshima (Japan, 1976)

Koumiko Mystery, The (Le Mystère Koumiko), dir. Chris Marker (France, 1965)

Liberal War, The, dir. Nick MacDonald (USA, 1972)

Living (Ikiru), dir. Akira Kurosawa (Japan, 1952)

Lower Depths, The (Donzoko), dir. Akira Kurosawa (Japan, 1957)

Man Vanishes, A (Ningen johatsu), dir. Shohei Imamura (Japan, 1967)

Memphis Belle, dir. William Wyler (USA, 1944)

Minamata: The Victims of the World (Minamata: Kanja-sans to sono sekai), dir. Noriaki Tsuchimoto (Japan, 1972)

Night and Fog (Nuit et brouillard), dir. Alain Resnais (France, 1955)

Night and Fog in Japan (Nihon no yoru to kiri), dir. Nagisa Oshima (Japan, 1960)

Nosferatu, the Vampire (Nosferatu–Eine Symphonie des Grauens), dir. F. W. Murnau (Germany, 1922)

Nosferatu, the Vampire (Nosferatu–Phantom der Nacht), dir. Werner Herzog (W. Germany, 1979)

Profound Desires of the Gods, The (Kamigami no fukaki yokuba), dir. Shohei Imamura (Japan, 1968)

Rashomon, dir. Akira Kurosawa (Japan, 1950)

Rebecca, dir. Alfred Hitchcock (USA, 1940)

Sans soleil, dir. Chris Marker (France, 1983)

Seven Samurai, The (Shichinin no samurai), dir. Akira Kurosawa (Japan, 1954)

Shoeshine (Sciuscia), dir. Vittorio de Sica (Italy, 1946)

Sympathy for the Devil (One Plus One), dir. Jean-Luc Godard (Great Britain, 1968)

Tokyo Story (Tokyo monogatari), dir. Yasujiro Ozu (Japan, 1953)

Touch of Evil, dir. Orson Welles (USA, 1958)

Vertigo, dir. Alfred Hitchcock (USA, 1958)

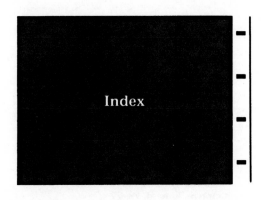

Index

Lightning Source UK Ltd.
Milton Keynes UK
26 March 2011

169922UK00001B/54/P